Born Again

Sandra Salinas Newton

Contents

The Timeless Ether

"Nightsky" - Image by vekstock on Freepik

Before I was yanked unceremoniously – without so much as a *kyrie eleison* – from that unwilling womb by a pair of cold and coarse hands, I was a sparkling star in the sky. Here is endless, restless speculation. Here is nowhere and everywhere at once. Here, I sleep and wake continually like the tide; dreams merge with reality until everything is hardly more than a thin gauze of blurred ideas.

We are all yearning for release into the world of corporeal bodies because this formlessness is pain. We ache to act out what we are upon supple and unsuspecting flesh. Or so I believe that the others here crave as I do. Else why would we share this shapeless, eternal prison?

I am Dionysus, once alive and vibrant, glimpsed imperfectly by those who, blind with wine and suffused with lust, have adored me. Yet, my origins were less than spectacular.

My father, Zeus, intended me to be his heir, successor to his infinite kingdom, yet this plan was foiled by his jealous wife, Hera, who opposed the crowning of a bastard who was both her grandson and her stepson because of her husband's unrelenting desires.

Zeus knew no boundaries. He was, after all, the God of gods, he who had, in a fierce ten-year battle, defeated the legendary Titans and imprisoned them deep in the bowels of Hell. Thus did Zeus and his Olympians come to power.

But such mastery creates its own weakness, and Zeus, in his pride, shed all his inhibitions to satisfy whatever he desired. So he reinforced his power by taking as lovers and consorts his own sisters, both Hera and Demeter. However, aware of the prevailing social strictures, even among the gods, he often disguised himself before committing his indiscretions, hoping thus to avoid his first wife's displeasure and certain revenge.

Thus, it was with Rhea's daughter, Demeter, Zeus' own niece and stepdaughter at once, for Rhea was his sister and his consort. His desire frightened Demeter, who turned herself into a snake to escape him. Zeus took the form of a snake as well, and the two intertwined as serpents; the resulting issue was a gentle girl they named Persephone. And here begins my story.

Or, almost. Zeus' brother, Hades, god of the underworld, saw my mother walking on earth and immediately kidnapped her, giving her delicious pomegranates to entice her to stay with him. Persephone's mother, my grandmother, missed her daughter so much, however, that she entreated the assistance of Zeus. Unable to completely secure my mother's release, he managed a compromise with his brother: Persephone would stay in the underworld with Hades for half the year and be reunited with her mother for the other half of the year.

Ah, but my mother was no simple pawn in this farce, for she so loved those pomegranates, fruits born of the underworld, that she returned to Hades willingly for half the year, basking contently in his love and eating his juicy fruit, not caring that her mother suffered so. There are always limits to our love, I suppose.

Persephone's coupling with Hades was not without its own complications. Their daughter, Melinoë, brought nightmares and madness to humans. And Persephone, like her mother, found herself the object of Zeus' attention. No need to prolong this trite tale: I was born as the first Dionysus, who Zeus intended to be his successor.

But Hera would not brook this. While she distracted me with infants' toys, she incited the Titans to dismember and devour me. Taking pity on me in my helpless infancy, Athena, the goddess of wisdom, snatched my heart away and brought it to Zeus, who made it into a potion by which he impregnated Semele, a human princess.

Further machinations occurred, not the least of which was Semele bursting into flames when she demanded to see Zeus in his true form. He rescued me from her womb and implanted me in his thigh until I was born. Thus was my truly first rebirth, sprung from violence and tragedy.

So I entered into the cycle of renewal, to be celebrated as

the successor to Zeus yet cursed as the one never to attain his due. And so I understand, as I wait here in the ether for a proper body to inhabit, that my thirst for my destiny cannot easily be slaked, and I must seek what satisfaction I may from these frail and transient bodies.

Inchcolm Abbey (MacGibbon and Ross)

Introducing Malcolm Joseph Murray

I had the world's attention the moment I emerged, bloody and bawling, from my mother's maw. That stupid cow of a midwife yanked me into the world by my ears, and while roughly wiping the slime of my mother off me, she noticed my twisted foot, saying, "God's blood, he's cursed." Then, to seal my fate as an outsider, as she was scrubbing my face with a filthy rag, she noticed my lazy eye that seemed to float in rather than glare at the world. "Pity us," she whispered, making sure that my mother, half-conscious, did not hear. But I heard her, and I would come to develop a glare that made others shiver.

"Malcolm," my mother murmured when she was told her newborn was a boy. So was I named, only later adding a second name – Joseph – after my father. Discretion directed them to bestow on me my mother's family name, Murray, because, of course, men who took holy orders were chaste and celibate, never violating a woman. Bishop Joseph remained prudently in the background, only sending some cakes and ale to my mother a week after my birth, ostensibly to celebrate my baptism, performed grudgingly by the local priest at the bishop's command.

The town of Inverkeithing did not regard me well. First of all, the midwife made sure to tell everyone she knew (and in a town so small, who did she not know?) of my infirmities. Second, my mother had already earned the shame of her family and the whole village because of her impropriety. It didn't matter that she had resisted ("not enough," her father pronounced) or that she had previously been beyond reproach ("too pretty not to go bad", the town gossip asserted). Besides, all the bad that was thought of her seemed to prove true when I arrived in so imperfect physical condition, for no perfectly formed child could issue from such a fallen woman. Yet, no one dared suggest I be done away with – drowned or smothered – because the fact remained that I was also the issue of a holy man, a bishop, and therefore *intactus*, untouchable and immune from assertive harm. Thus, Malcolm Joseph Murray joined the world at large.

The Murray family's local wealth was a source of petty

jealousy, so they had the unenviable position of being almost middle-class in the small enclave of Inverkeithing. Situated on the Firth of Ford in Fife, Scotland, it is about sixteen kilometers from Edinburgh, a thriving port town, and my mother's family owned the sole ship-breaking firm. My grandfather had been astute enough to realize that sailing ships have a recognizable lifespan and, therefore, can be bought cheaply when old or damaged. In turn, these retired vessels could be salvaged for parts to be refurbished and resold for a good price. And Inverkeithing, being so near Edinburgh, was well-situated because while Edinburgh was crowded with mercantile ships doing brisk trade, a short trip up the Ford to Inverkeithing was convenient for those wishing to rid themselves of ships barely sea-worthy.

When I was a young lad, I thought myself perfectly suited to the Murray family business. Like their discarded ships, I was imperfect. Yet, I was also, like their ships, still useful. I could, as the son of the only surviving issue of Grandfather Murray (three sisters and two brothers had not survived infancy, leaving my mother an only and treasured child), learn the business with an eye to eventually inheriting it. My infirmities would be overlooked, I was sure. But I was soon disabused of that notion.

"Yer a bastard, nothin' will change that," Grandfather proclaimed. "I'll make sure my daughter is cared for, but she must teach yer to fend for yerself."

I stood in a corner of the old man's office, surprised by his decision. It was all the more disappointing as it was declared today on my twelfth birthday. "Yes, Grandfather," I whispered, knowing I could not convince him otherwise.

"Perhaps yer true Da will do something for yer; he certainly has done nothing for yer poor mother." Grandfather Murray cleared his throat with disgust. The very thought of Bishop Joseph put Grandfather in rumbling fits of coughing.

As I was slipping out of the room, Grandfather was muttering between his hacking coughs: "Malcolm, indeed! A king's name for a gutter child." If he noticed that I was gone, he was probably relieved.

It was that day I realized I would be on my own unless something changed. My mother was useless. Perhaps she had always been. She was a simpering girl whose virginity was easily if cruelly snatched in a single encounter with the lascivious Bishop. Grandfather had presented himself before the ecclesiastical court in a local dispute. He'd brought his wife and daughter to the hearing because he thought it might garner him more sympathy for his cause. His wife was old beyond her years (the birthing of six children and the subsequent death of five of them wore heavily on her), but his daughter, just thirteen, exhibited all the promise of the Murray family: beauty, sweet temperament, and even some native intelligence.

After the Bishop ruled in Grandfather Murray's favor, he showed up at the old man's door that evening, where he was welcomed heartily; he had, after all, saved Grandfather a small fortune. To Bishop Joseph, it did not matter who was right or wrong. The young girl's radiant beauty swayed him easily to the Murray side.

After some glasses of scotch, the Bishop inquired, "Is this girl your only child?" He glanced at her, sitting in a shadowed corner next to her dozing mother.

"Yessir," Grandfather answered. "Katie is the only surviving child of six total. We treasure her mightily." The old man yawned; the day's excitement and the scotch fatigued him.

"And has she been baptized and confirmed in Holy Mother Church?" the bishop inquired, watching the girl's soft body glimmer in the candlelight.

"Baptized, yes, of course. Confirmed no. We've been overwhelmed with the deaths of her siblings and have wanted only to keep her healthy and safe."

"I can do the rite for you immediately if you'd like. I would only ask that you donate something to the Church in gratitude." The Bishop already fingered his rosary with anticipation.

Grandfather had looked at his wife, but she was asleep in her chair, snoring softly. He nodded. "Yer would surely honor us, Bishop. And I would be glad to give something for the Church's trouble."

"Good, good. Show me where you pray, and I'll confirm the girl there." Bishop Joseph rose from the table and drank the last of the scotch in his glass. He smoothed the folds of his cassock and patted down his bright pink *zuchetto*, the beanie which all ecclesiastics were privileged to wear.

Grandfather stood and walked to a doorway. "Here," he pointed. "We pray in the bedroom under the crucifix that hangs above the armoire. It is a private alcove for my wife and me. Shall I accompany you?"

"No, just get the donation and lay it here on the table. Then, pour some scotch into a dish; it will serve as the anointing liquid tonight once I bless it. Finally, stay here to make sure your wife doesn't wake up and disturb the rite. I'll take your daughter – Katie, is it? – to the makeshift altar." The bishop could not believe the man's stupidity and gullibility.

Grandfather nodded. "I'll fetch the donation in a moment." He poured the scotch into the dish and carefully handed it to the Bishop, turning to an old clay pot on a shelf for the coins.

I'd heard this story many times from both my Grandfather and Grandmother: how they had given hospitality to the Bishop, grateful for his ruling in their case. How Grandmother could not help falling asleep. How Grandfather, having drunk too much, thought the Bishop's offer a gracious proposal, for his daughter would have a private Confirmation by the esteemed Bishop Joseph. It would surely raise his standing in Inverkeithing.

The rest of the story I had to hear from my mother whenever she was overcome with sadness or scorned by neighbors or scolded by her parents. In other words, she told me her story almost every night as if it were a lullaby meant to ease me to sleep.

He took me into the bedroom, a narrow, dark room crowded with their bed, a chair, and a small, crude wooden armoire that was a wedding gift to my mother from her parents. The bishop led me to the armoire where he told me to kneel. In fact, he helped me gently, holding my hand so I would not lose my balance.

He placed the dish holding a puddle of scotch on the armoire, then pulled the chair in front of where I was kneeling. It was a small space: he could easily reach over my head to the dish, which he did after seating himself in the chair. "Close your eyes, child," he said, touching first my eyelids with the tips of his fingers, then my nose, then my lips. The scotch burned my skin, and I jerked back.

"You must remain still," Bishop Joseph whispered. He pulled my head forward into his knees, holding me securely against him. "Do you know the Confirmation prayer?"

My head was pressed against the rough cloth of his cassock so I could not speak. I only shook my head.

Bishop Joseph patted my head. "All right, just say it in your mind as I speak the words for you," he directed. "*Holy Spirit, confirm in me. Holy Spirit, you are the giver of many gifts which God wants to give me very personally.*" He stopped and groaned. "*Open my heart and my mind as I prepare for Confirmation.*"

Suddenly, he lifted me into an upright position and pulled me to him, wrapping one arm around my waist. Fumbling with the other hand in the tight space between us, he then lifted my skirt. His hand found my private part and closed on it. "Now, child, say the prayer aloud after me: *Help me to know that you are confirming all the goodness that I am.*" He looked into my eyes.

I trembled. "Help me to know that you are confirming all the goodness that I am," I repeated in a small whisper. Then I gasped.

His hand led his penis inside me. Sudden. Abrupt. Unexpected. And Hasty. Hoarsely, as he jerked forward rudely, he finished the prayer: "*. . . and all the goodness that I will be-come.*" With a final spasm, he withdrew from me and sat down, at the same time pushing me to my knees. "You are sweet good-ness, child," he said, sighing. "And I name you Joan, warrior of God."

I lowered my head. I could feel blood dribbling down my leg, so I squeezed my thighs together, hoping to catch the drip-ping. My hands were on the bishop's knees.

He patted my hands gently. Then, he lifted my face to him, keeping his hand under my chin. "*Benedico tibi et con-firmo te, carissime fili*" he said – "I bless you and confirm you, dear child" – and slapped me across my face. "You are now a soldier for Christ." He pushed his chair back and stood up, straightening his cassock and his *zuchetto*. He smiled briefly at me and said, "Not a word, child. Go somewhere and clean your-self. You have bled for God and your reward will surely be heaven." He left the room.

"I waited until I heard him speaking with my father, thanking him for the donation, and then closing the door be-hind him. When he was gone, I wiped my legs with the edge of my skirt dabbed in the dish of scotch. I carried the dish back out to the table.

When father saw me, he poked at mother and said to her, "Our daughter has been confirmed in the bosom of Mother Church now. The bishop has confirmed her name to be Joan. We need not worry about her anymore." And they went wearily to bed.

When Mother finished her story, she would lay next to me, cuddle close, and say in my ear, "With your crippled leg and your evil eye, you are the Bishop's constant warning to me to bear my sin in shame." That was, in fact, the prayer that put both of us to sleep every night. I did not put a name to it then, but I knew that my mother had descended into madness and would never return.

Leaving Inverkeithing

My grandfather's dislike of me and my mother's insanity were facts of my childhood and, as such, didn't really bother me. My club foot and lazy eye were the same: simple facts. As a child, I simply accepted the facts of my life. I was quietly baptized one Saturday night soon after my birth in the dark hollow of St. Peter in Chains' baptismal font, with my grandparents serving as godparents and my mother softly weeping in a pew. The priest performed the baptism only because he had been so ordered by Bishop Joseph. When the rite was finished, we were ushered out, and the door unceremoniously barred behind us. We retired to the Murray home, where no celebration awaited us; a wetnurse gave me her cold teat for supper while my relatives ate their dinner in silence.

I was not tormented by anyone: the "facts" of my life effectively kept me apart from the townspeople. They avoided me, kept their children away from me, and left me alone. I did not suffer at their hands, but neither did I find comfort in their company.

By age twelve, I had no experience of the wider world and little experience of even my birthplace. Inverkeithing was where I lived, but I knew it not at all. If I'd been dropped from the sky onto one of its narrow streets, I would have been completely lost. My life was lived within the confines of the Murray property: a modest house, some fields grazed by sheep, and some outbuildings on the edge of the water where Grandfather had his office, storage barns, and ship-breaking yards. The only people of Inverkeithing I saw were some servants, shepherds, and laborers.

I didn't go to school; my grandmother occasionally read to me from her Bible, allowing me to sit close by and follow her finger as it underlined the words on the thin pages. She would only read from the books of Law of the Old Testament, those pages which recounted God's creation and the rules He imposed to insure righteous living. This was how I acquired a rudimentary ability to read, connecting sound to sight. And when

Grandfather saw that I could read, albeit barely, he grudgingly taught me to write my name. Thus, I could claim, with some grandiosity, at age twelve that I was capable of reading and writing. Luckily, no one challenged me to prove it. Otherwise, they would have discovered that my skills were quite limited.

Every boy craves companionship, some kind of society to which he can claim membership. In this, I was no different. But, I remained isolated from any real connection to people, and my search for company led ultimately to the sheep in the fields. I learned to observe from afar where the shepherds led their flocks (Grandfather allowed grazing for a small monthly fee) and where the shepherds themselves sat or left their flock unattended. I would find a more secluded spot in some tall grass near the herd and wait with a pocketful of corn. A single sheep would eventually find its way to me, enticed by the corn to remain close by. Then, I would tell that sheep the stories that had been told me: grandmother's recitals of the books of the Bible and my mother's nightly recitation of her assault. The sheep were never judgmental, requiring only some corn to listen patiently. Sometimes, I was able to nuzzle a sheep's matted curls, its earthen odor signifying security and constancy to me.

I spent hours in those fields, laying on my back watching the clouds travel through the skies, listening to the soft conversations of the sheep, and observing their wooly society reacting to the changes in seasons. I saw sheep argue, fight over tufts of grass, court one another rudely by sniffing one another's odors, and create bonds of affection such as between mother and lambkin. From them, I learned the elements of socialization.

One day, when I was thirteen, I noted that a shepherd had driven his herd to the usual spot but was himself not alone. Instead, he was accompanied by a girl who, by her dress, was a farmer's daughter. Her clothes were clean but rough-made, home-sewn, probably by her mother. She was a plump girl, her wide hips clearly delineating her shape under her dress. I crept closer.

"So, does yer father know where yer are?" the shepherd asked, sitting next to her on the gentle slope from which they could see the sheep grazing. I was behind them, invisible.

"Nah," she laughed coarsely, "he don't care."

The shepherd pushed her down onto the grass and rolled on top of her. "And if he finds out?"

"He'll kill yer unless yer marry me." She laughed again, hugging him and wrapping her legs around him.

"I've got nothing better to do. Now, let me sample yer." He pushed himself up on his arms, giving the girl space to un-wrap him from her legs and, instead, pull up her skirts and spread her legs.

"I'll want a kiss, too," she said, closing her eyes.

I watched them with curiosity. I had seen the sheep mate; it was not an act unfamiliar to me. But this position – the two facing one another, talking, her asking for a kiss – was new to me. It excited me. And when they seemed to be most enjoying themselves, moaning and crying out with sounds of pleasure, I also climaxed for the first time. I had been on my stomach, ob-serving the couple. Now, I rolled over on my back, out of breath and feeling spent. I smiled. It was a wonderful experience. I qui-etly crawled away from them to find one of my usual spots for observing the flock, but this time, I fell asleep and did not wake for many hours, feeling refreshed and satisfied.

That observation of the shepherd and his girl aroused my curiosity about other humans. However, I was not to be re-warded with more observations of the kind that I had witnessed that day. The house servants, all women, simply went about their tasks and then left for their own homes at the end of the day. The men working the discarded ships did the same. I had no opportunity to observe interactions between men and women. So, I had no recourse except to make inquiries of my relatives.

"Where do children come from?" was not the right ques-tion to ask my mother. It sent her into a full day of crying and moaning. I moved on to my grandmother. Her reply was simple but not very informative: "The same place as calves and lamb-kins and all living creatures, God's goodness." When I posed the question to my grandfather, he looked hard at me and said, "We'll be talking soon, Malcolm. First, I need to consult with that bastard, the Bishop."

It was months before Grandfather Murray could get an audience with Bishop Joseph, and it was arranged to be held at the Bishop's seat in Edinburgh. Grandfather was told to speak to the parish priest about the requirements of the meeting itself.

Father Philip was a spare and sour man. His idea of priesthood was to teach his parish how to keep to the narrow path of righteousness by scolding and berating. As a result, few liked him, and they contributed to the church of St. Peter in Chains the very least they could get away with. The church was old and small, renovated at various points from the time it was founded in the fifth century. Now, in the 1200s, it was larger but still dark and somber, a place seemingly made for repentance and atonement rather than for jubilation and celebration. Narrow windows lined the side walls but lacked stained glass or, indeed, any covering at all, so in winter, the church was even more depressing. Its namesake, St. Peter Ad Vincula, had been fortunate to be rescued by an angel from his imprisonment by Herod, but the architecture of this place was created more to reflect that imprisonment rather than Peter's liberation.

"Bishop Joseph sent word to me that I was to instruct yer on yer behavior when yer meet with him in Edinburgh," Father Philip said, addressing not only my grandfather but me as well. We were seated in the front pews.

"Yes, yes, as if I didn't have manners," Grandfather grumbled.

"First, yer must make a contribution to the Church for my time and knowledge," Father Philip said, boldly holding out his hand.

Grandfather sneered but reached into his pocket and dropped two coins into the priest's palm. "I expected such. Get on with it."

The priest smiled sourly. "The bishop must be addressed as 'His Eminence.' Never address him directly. Don't turn yer back on him at any time, for it shows great disrespect. Never interrupt him when he's speaking. Only sit if he invites it. And wear clean clothes that don't smell. He's very particular about odors." The priest stopped. "Can yer remember all that?"

Grandfather nodded. "Not to worry. I'll be sure to follow all yer instructions. Anything else?" He stood up to leave, clearly anxious to rid himself of the church's atmosphere as well as of the priest himself.

"Yes, the most important." The priest looked directly at me. "There's nothing yer can do about his crippled foot, but be sure to dress him in a clean leine and trousers. And for Edinburgh, he'll need footwear."

I stepped back, suddenly conscious of the short pants and baggy shirt that was my common dress. I had no shoes.

"It's not my habit to spoil the bastard with clothing," Grandfather grumbled.

"We're not speaking of what yer want," the priest replied. "And one last thing." He took a deep breath.

"What?" Grandfather said loudly and impatiently.

"Yer must cover that evil eye of his. A leather patch will do nicely."

I involuntarily touched my eye. I blushed.

"It shall be done as required," Grandfather agreed.

When we left, the priest was standing in the church's doorway with his arms folded across his chest. He had acted in character, giving instruction to his ignorant flock. I didn't need to look back; his eyes followed me sternly.

"I'll have my wife prepare yer clothes. But yer must get yerself to my leatherman at the stables in town. His name is Gregory. Tell him yer from the Murray family and that I need two things. First, he must have horses and a carriage with the driver at my house in two days' time for a trip to Edinburgh.

Second, and this must be done immediately while yer wait, he's to fashion a patch for that cursed eye of yers. Make sure it fits snug, and the leather is thick. I'll settle with him when we return from Edinburgh."

I stood, not moving in the small square in front of the church. I was stunned that Grandfather was entrusting an errand to me. It was the first time he'd done so.

"Well?" he said, stamping his foot. "Do yer expect angels to carry yer?"

I shook my head then whispered, "Where is these stables, Grandfather?"

The old man took me by the shoulders, turned me to face the east street, and pushed me forward. "There. Walk there until yer see the stables. Talk to Gregory. Go!"

I stumbled forward, then began to walk briskly. I didn't dare turn around. Inverkeithing is not very big, so I came upon the stables within minutes and, one hour later, emerged with a brown leather patch over my eye and tied with a leather band at the back of my head.

I was impressed with how the name Murray turned my requests to Gregory into what seemed like commands that he could not refuse. Of course, he knew I was the illegitimate issue of the Murray daughter, for no one else in town had my appearance or history. So, I enjoyed the deference with which I was being treated, not realizing that a good part of it was revulsion dressed up in courtesy.

At first, I had trouble walking steadily with the patch over my eye. It threw off my balance and my depth perception. Still, I found my way back to the Church and, from there, could easily walk home. But when I reached the small pond at the edge of the Murray property and looked at my reflection, I could not help but smile. I looked mysterious, I thought. How much better would I seem once new clothes were added!

Arriving in Edinburgh

I had two days before the journey to Bishop Joseph and Edinburgh. Grandfather would not tell me why we were seeing the bishop despite my asking him numerous times. He would simply answer, "Yer'll see" or "I'm busy, can't yer see?" So, I was left to speculate on my own.

Of course, I wondered if the meeting had anything to do with my asking Grandfather about where children came from. Having had no companions my own age in my whole life and having around me only adults who preferred I simply stay out of their way, I lacked any notion of common human interactions. My mother's story of having been attacked by the bishop made sense to me only up to a point. I couldn't say I understood everything she'd described, and her overwhelming madness prevented questions of clarification. Simply, I was ignorant.

After much speculation that I kept to myself, I decided that it didn't matter if I knew the purpose of the visit to the bishop in Edinburgh. I determined to make the visit valuable for myself: I would take in the sights, learn about Edinburgh as much as I could, and, most importantly, impress the Bishop somehow. From what I could figure, he was my sire, although that meant nothing to me.

So, he was my sire. So what? The rams and bulls who sired lambs and calves were instruments or tools by which life was created, nothing more. The only connections I saw were between mothers and offspring; the sires simply performed a service, although I could not say I understood how the coupling led to the appearance of offspring sometime later. The only hint I had that it was different from humans was my Grandfather's apparent affection for his daughter, my mother. He protected her, which his wife, being frail, could not do. He pitied her madness. So, perhaps the bishop would protect me, pity me? But from what? For what?

Overwhelmed with such questions, I spent these last two days in Inverkeithing doing only two things: reciting Biblical passages and enjoying a new-found vanity. As to the latter, my grandmother had found an old but decent leine of grandfather's. The linen had lost its crispness and bright hue, but it served, along with a supple leather belt, as an acceptable shirt-like tunic for me. This outfit, which I was ordered not to wear until our day of departure, along with my eyepatch, made me feel almost handsome. In addition, she hastily sewed me a pair of felt shoes, lined with stiff cutouts of wooly lambs hide and tied with braided threads, making sure to make the insole of one of the shoes especially thick, so my limping clubfoot was not so noticeable. Whenever I passed by any reflective surface – a pond, a puddle, a freshly-scrubbed dish – I looked at myself and smiled; I could not resist the charm of having lost my evil eye behind a piece of leather.

Reciting Bible passages was more difficult, but I'd decided that my ability to do so would impress the Bishop enough for him to like me, if not show me some affection. For these last two days, I pestered Grandmother to say aloud to me her favorite Bible excerpts; I would make sure to get her to repeat these excerpts over and over by complimenting her and telling her how inspiring the words were to me. I depended on my good ear for mimicry that allowed me to commit to memory what she'd recite. By the morning of my departure, I had two or three quotations I could reasonably and convincingly recite as if I had memorized them myself as if I had actually read them.

Expecting the trip to take under three hours, Grandfather and I left at six a.m. on a sunny Saturday morning. We would not hurry the horses, and we expected the roads to be busy since it was a market day. We hoped that our business with the bishop would be finished in an hour's time, so we estimated being back in Inverkeithing by supper or a bit later. At any rate, Grandfather said he wanted to be in his own bed that night.

I was disappointed that Grandfather had not planned to stay overnight in Edinburgh. All I would see of the city would be from the seat of the carriage, it seemed, and I would not be allowed the time or space to stand among strangers, hear their conversations, smell their city odors, rub against their urban skin. We were barely out of Inverkeithing itself, and my expectations were already keenly thwarted.

We saw others on the road: carts loaded with vegetables or lumber on the way to market, bundles of wool and hay for use in the city, and people in small groups of two or four riding or walking the wide, dusty road to Edinburgh. The sight of all these people amazed me, but no more than when we finally reached Edinburgh, where, for me, the world converged like a seething river of bodies, noises, and colors.

"Close yer mouth before yer dribble on yerself," Grandfather said with some annoyance at my naivete while he urged our driver forward. "Don't mind these jackasses in the road."

The bishop's residence was a grand affair, at least to my eyes: a low stone building set back from the road, fronted with gardens of heather. The façade was lined with wide windows on both sides of a double-door entry. The gate was not guarded, but emblazoned in the black wrought iron were Latin words: *Dominus Deus Pastor Noster Est.*

"Find a stable for the carriage and an inn for a meal for yerself," Grandfather told the driver, handing him a thin purse of coins. "Come back in two hours and don't be late." He turned to me, urging me forward to enter the grounds of the residence.

Inside the vestibule, at the end of which were glassed doors to a garden, a priest bade us sit while he quietly slipped into one of the four doorways to tell the Bishop we had arrived. Our chairs were padded with silver-embroidered cloth and looked luxurious, but to me, the seats were hard and unyielding and seemed to have been made only to look comfortable. The cavernous hall was hushed, so noises from the street drifted in: horses neighing and drivers shouting curses, the clatter of cartwheels, the clashing of boxes against one another on the bumpy road – all combining into a steady drone of commotion. As fascinated as I was, I felt the insistent throb of a headache and wished I were back in an Inverkeithing field, hearing the low murmurs of sheep and the whispers of breezes gently moving the clouds overhead.

The door to our left opened, and the priest who had ushered us to seats now motioned for us to follow him into the room. Grandfather rose with some effort – I thought the chair had been uncomfortable for him, too – and pulled me up by an elbow. "Now's the time, Malcolm," he said.

I expected a lavish room of silks and brocades, a huge golden desk, and a hundred stark-white candles burning brightly. "Remain standing," the priest whispered to us, "until the bishop comes forward. Then, you must kneel and kiss his ring. Show humility." The priest stepped back into the shadows but did not leave the room. The room was stark in comparison to what I expected.

There was a fireplace, empty now because it was late Spring. In front of the fireplace, four wing chairs faced one another in an irregular circle, and a round maroon rug lay inside the circle. There were two small rectangular tables, one for each pair of chairs, on which stood tiny crucifixes. The wall above the fireplace was hung with a dark banner into which was woven a representation of Christ in the night garden of Gethsemane. To the left, an alcove with a kneeling bench, and to the right, a small desk, lantern, and low bookcase overflowing with books, scrolls, and loose pages. It was *austere*.

"It's good to see you again, Master Murray," the bishop said, moving forward. When he reached us, he put out his right hand, the fingers curled inward, presenting his bishop's ring to us.

Grandfather went down on a single knee, genuflecting instead of kneeling, and touched the ring briefly with his lips. He did not kiss it, exactly. He stayed on one knee but did not bow his head after.

I dropped onto both my knees so quickly that I felt one knee bruising on the hardwood floor. I kissed the ring after wetting my lips with my tongue and noticed that I'd left a bit of spittle on the deep purple amethyst protruding from the center of the gold ring. I bowed my head and closed my eyes, hoping he would not notice my sloppy kiss. I mumbled: "The Lord is gracious, slow to anger and bountiful in love." I waited.

Bishop Joseph hesitated, then chuckled. "A pleasant surprise that you know scripture. Come, sit down." He walked back into the room toward the chairs.

Grandfather growled a little but hoisted himself upright and followed the bishop. "Hurry on, brat," he muttered to me, clearly annoyed with my scripture quoting.

We settled into the chairs. The bishop motioned to the priest in the shadows, who quickly appeared with a small chalice of wine. "My daily constitutional," the bishop explained, sipping lightly at the red liquid but pointedly not offering us any. "I understand you want to talk about the boy," he said, nodding toward me.

"As is only right," Grandfather insisted. "He is past thirteen. I think it's time, yer Eminence," he added with no small irony.

"I'm under no obligation, you understand." The bishop smiled. He had crossed his legs, and I noticed his slippers were red silk with golden braided drawstrings at the ankles. I wondered if they would fit me and how they would feel on my calloused feet.

"Perhaps not by law, but by what yer done to my daughter," Grandfather insisted in a hard voice.

"I am sorry she was so frail, but she is blessed with a child of God," the bishop responded.

"A child – his name is Malcolm Joseph Murray for His Holiness's information – which she cannot care for, who is disliked by the town for his mother's sins, and who I think should be acknowledged by his father."

"Murray, you say?" the bishop narrowed his eyes. "If that's his surname, then his paternity is beyond acknowledging, I think." His face did not reveal the pleasure he felt when he heard that I had also been named after him, albeit with only a middle name. He sipped at his wine and looked at me. "Why do you have a patch on your eye, son?"

I thrilled at the word *son*, too stupid to realize he did not mean it literally. I smiled. "Grandfather had the man at the stables make it to cover my evil eye." I carelessly flipped up the patch to reveal my eye that refused to match the motions of its mate, as if it were too lazy to do so. Then, I covered it again and smiled.

"It isn't so evil so much as it seems independent, following its own rules. Keep it covered, boy; ignorant people will make more of it than you want." He turned to Grandfather. "Now, Master Murray, what else is wrong with the boy that you would impose him on me as if I had some blame in his birth?"

"His foot is twisted and the leg short. He's the perfect example of sins of the fathers." Grandfather shifted in the chair but stared coldly at the bishop.

I had not really been following the conversation very closely, more interested in the Bishop himself and his wonderful surroundings. But when I heard the tail-end of Grandfather's words, I instinctively chimed in: "The sins of the fathers are visited upon the children." I had only one more memorized Bible verse, and I had to make sure that using it would impress the bishop.

Bishop Joseph looked toward me with anger but then shrugged his shoulders. "Children learn words more easily than meanings, eh?"

"Sometimes, the meanings don't need learning; they are readily understood." Grandfather answered.

The bishop sighed. "All right, Murray," he said, pointedly addressing Grandfather without the honorific now. "Shall I take the misfit off your hands? What can I do with him?"

"Well, I can't have him. None of my people will work beside him. I will not include him in my daughter's inheritance. When she dies, he will be cast out, I assure you. I have no use for someone who reminds me of the dissolution of my family."

"Does he have any skill at anything?" the bishop asked.

"He can read a little, Joseph," Grandfather answered,

dropping the bishop's honorific in kind, "and write his name. So, I guess it means he's no idiot."

"If you want me to help him, you must show me the respect due me as a religious," the bishop warned, straightening in his chair.

"Then, Bishop Joseph," Grandfather agreed, " we are agreed."

"I will put him in a monastery to learn more. There, at least, his physical shortcomings will be overlooked as long as his brain shows promise."

"Thank you, then, yer Eminence." Grandfather rose to shake the bishop's hand, a common sign of agreement.

The bishop rose. Instead of taking Grandfather's hand, he proffered his own with the great, sparkling amethyst ring. "This is the way of the Holy Mother Church," he explained.

Grandfather nodded, genuflected, and kissed the ring. "I'll have a word with Malcolm, please, Bishop Joseph."

"Of course. When you're done, the priest will show you out. God bless you, Murray." The bishop briefly blessed Grandfather then hurried out.

I had watched the proceedings with curiosity. Half the time, however, I was not paying attention, desiring instead to look more closely at the room or its furnishings, at the bishop or at the priest standing silently in the shadows. And, always cognizant of the noises drifting in from the street, I wanted to go outside and explore.

Grandfather pulled me by my shoulders to my feet. "I'll say my goodbyes now, Malcolm. Yer understand that yer're to stay with Bishop Joseph from now on, doing whatever he says. He is, after all, yer father."

"My father?" I echoed emptily. Was there a point to having a father? "What about my ma?"

"Yer know she's sick," Grandfather said. "And when she hears yer gone, I'm sure she'll cry herself to death, which is better for her overall." The old man looked into my eyes. "Yer understand, yeah?" He didn't wait for my answer. "Yer was with yer mother. Now it's time to be with yer father." Grandfather stated baldly. "Don't give him a hard time, Malcolm. He's yer dad." Then Grandfather patted my shoulders and straightened my clothes. He put a small pearl in my hand. "This was to be yer mother's one day if she married. I hope yer'll be happy one day." He sighed, then turned to the priest, "Get me out of this sinner's paradise."

I blurted out the last verse I'd memorized: "You shall love your neighbor as yourself."

Grandfather grunted. "That's a fool's errand. Goodbye, Malcolm."

I was left alone in the room. Without thinking, I put the pearl in my shoe. The room was, itself, almost as big as Grandfather's house. I wondered if I was to live here. The rug seemed cozy enough to sleep on, especially when a fire could be lit in winter.

The priest reappeared. "Bishop Joseph wishes me to oversee your management until we can settle you in a monastery. My name is Father Julian. I'm sure you have questions, but for now, let's get you a room, more appropriate clothes for a bishop's nephew, and some food, eh?"

"Nephew?" I asked. I didn't even know what a nephew was.

"It's how you'll be introduced from now on. Come along."

I was shown to a room at the back of the house and down a small flight of steps. It was one of two rooms situated below ground level. There were no windows, and the room was plain, clean, and quiet. It contained a single bed covered with a sheet, pillow, and thin, gray blanket; a simple wooden chair; a plain prie-dieu; and a small table on which a candle and Bible had been placed. On one wall was a plank of five wooden hooks; two white linen leines and a pair of soft leather pants hung there. Leaning against that same wall was a pair of worn leather shoes and, next to that, a chamber pot.

"These are your clothes for the week; someone will launder them and provide clean clothes as replacements. The shoes will not be replaced, so take care of them. If you follow the stairs back up to the main floor and turn left, you'll find a small alcove with a basin, pitcher, and towel. Fill the basin in the garden pool to wash up and empty it afterwards as a courtesy to the rest of us in the house. And you should empty and clean out your chamber pot everyday as well. Do you have questions, Malcolm?" The priest stood in the doorway; he didn't seem anxious to go.

"Who else lives here?"

"The Bishop, of course. Me. And there's a cook and her helper who live on the other side of the house. I live in the room just across the hall."

"Father Julian, what's a chamber pot?" My head was spinning with everything new.

The young priest laughed. "Just call me Julian. It's that bowl over there by your shoes. It's for pissing and shitting, but you need to empty and clean it out with water daily."

"I've never seen such a thing," I said, truly amazed. I didn't have to go outside? How pleasant! "And what's a nephew?" I figured I should ask all my questions before Julian became annoyed with me.

"That's you. Don't ever think of yourself as anything but

Bishop Joseph's nephew, all right? If you do that, your life will be far better than it's been so far."

I couldn't help asking: "And if I don't?"

"There are worse places in the world than your stinking little Inverkeithing. Places where you will wake up every day in complete misery and pain. Places where you will not understand the language or the customs and where the only words spoken to you will be curses laid heavily on your head. Take heed, Malcolm, the Bishop is a powerful man and knows many other powerful men. He does not accept disobedience easily, and he carries grudges." With that, Julian turned away and pulled the door closed.

I was in Edinburgh, away from my solitary life in Inverkeithing. But Julian's warning frightened me. I did not think I could slip away so easily in my new situation.

Julian brought me my supper – a small bowl of soup and a piece of lamb with a bread crust – on a tray, explaining that the cook had not been informed there was a new resident, so this was all she could provide for tonight. He didn't stay to watch me eat, didn't ask if I had any other questions, but quickly left. "My supper'll be cold unless I get back," he said.

Without a window, I couldn't tell what time of day or night it was, so after I ate, I crept up the stairs with a chamber pot in hand and found the garden. I thought if anyone discovered me, I would say I was just emptying the pot out. Once I got to the garden, I placed the still-empty chamber pot just inside the doorway.

I wandered farther into the garden and found a stone bench near a small running fountain. The sky above me was dark. The stars seemed so far away, unlike the night sky in Inverkeithing. I had to admit I missed the old familiarity of the place; I felt insecure and uncertain here.

"Your supper will be better tomorrow, I promise," said Bishop Joseph, who had appeared before me like a ghost. His silk shoes, glimmering in the moonlight, had made no sound.

I stood up clumsily. "The food was fine, sir."

"Sit, sit. I didn't mean to startle you. Please don't ever forget that I am 'Your Eminence,' not 'Sir.' All right, Malcolm?" He spoke in a whisper so I had to lean in towards him to be sure I caught every word.

"Yes, your. . .your Eminence," I stumbled over the words and blushed, although I was sure he could not see in the dark garden.

His hand was suddenly on my cheek, a soft, slightly moist hand. "You're blushing! How charming!" He ran his hand down my face to my chin, which he lifted up so I would face him. "What do you know of the world, child?"

"Not a child any longer, according to Grandfather. But I know nothing, and I think that is why Grandfather brought me to you, so I could learn." I was relieved to admit what I thought was the point of my being here.

"Yes, to learn. Of course." His hand still cupped under my chin, he said softly, "Touch me, Malcolm."

Had I heard him correctly? I reached out and put my hand on his shoulder.

"Dear child," he said with amusement. His hand left my chin and reached out to take my hand on his shoulder. "Here," he said, pressing my hand into his lap.

My eyes widened, but I did not move: I neither pressed farther nor pulled back. I let my hand rest under his.

He pressed more and closed his eyes. "Do you feel that?" he asked.

"You mean your hand?" I asked. I did not want to talk about what I felt *under* my hand.

"Have you never enjoyed the pleasures of another? A man? A woman?" He lifted my hand and put two of my fingers in his mouth, sucking at them.

"Uh. . . ." I couldn't speak. I suddenly felt the same physical heat that I'd felt the day I spied on the couple in the field. "No, sir. . .uh. . . your. . .Em-eminence." Involuntarily, I moaned.

Bishop Joseph laughed, releasing my hand. "You are truly an innocent, not unlike your mother when I first came upon her." He laughed again, so heartily that he had to reach inside his cassock for his delicate white handkerchief to wipe the tears out of his eyes.

Uncomfortable, trying not to ejaculate as I had done once before, I shifted on the bench away from the bishop. I looked down, hoping my erection was not evident, and covered myself with my hand still wet from the bishop's mouth.

"Oh, you will certainly learn much here before I send you off. But I don't like to teach these things; I prefer those who already know what to do and how to do it. I'll leave it to Father Julian to teach you the mastery of pleasure. First, of course, he'll show you how to enjoy yourself. Be an attentive pupil, my son, and Julian will send you to me when you're ready." The bishop stood up and brushed off his cassock. "God bless, and good night."

He left me in the dark garden where the stars seemed so cold and far away. I retrieved the chamber pot and found my way back to my room where I lay on the bed stroking my eyepatch while I tried to understand what tomorrow might bring.

I needn't have thought about it too much. Aside from a dull routine of meals, daily prayers at my prie-dieu, and very brief readings from my Bible with Julian, each day was devoted to specific lessons suited, Julian asserted, to the time of day.

Mornings, right after I woke, Julian was there to encourage and heighten the erection I woke with; he said my erotic dreams should be enjoyed to their fullest by giving in to satisfying the erection. He massaged me and sometimes put his tongue in my mouth or bit my ear to make me climax. Then, almost offhandedly, he would wipe off his hands and say, "Go wash for breakfast."

Afternoons, the routine was just the opposite: I was to be the one to bring him to an erection and to climax. He taught me how to handle him, to touch him so it aroused him, and most importantly, how to derive my own pleasure from this role.

After supper with the Bishop, who spoke to me only of my Bible studies and my progress in reading scriptures, Julian would take me beyond the house into the streets of Edinburgh. He knew his way in the narrow alleys and past the boisterous taverns filled with light and music.

Sometimes, he found a girl in a dark street who he'd whisper to while I stood awkwardly in silence, and she would pleasure me quickly and expertly before counting the coins Julian dropped in her hand. Other times, he brought me to a particular house where an older woman greeted us familiarly and where I was led into a room and told to pleasure the girl laying apathetically on the bed. If she said afterwards that she was bored with me, she was paid, and we would leave; Julian would box my ears when we were in the street. If she said afterwards that I had pleased her, she would be paid the same, but Julian would also buy me a pastry on our way back to the house.

I don't want to give the impression that all of this was simply work for me. Although it puzzled me at first, and I thought it sinful because it was so clandestine, after a few weeks, I began to actually enjoy these lessons in carnality, and I challenged myself to become more expert at each aspect of these acts. Julian never told me that what we were doing was wrong or evil; he only admonished me not to speak about it because *others would not understand.* I understood what he said in the same way that I understood the way people judged me because of my infirmities. It was simply a fact of life. But Julian showed me that there are ways around such facts: keeping our own counsel, we could enjoy our lives freely and privately. We could laugh in our sleeves about the stupid small-mindedness of others. I was thrilled at the idea that I was somehow *better* than others.

It was a little over six months before I was summoned to the Bishop's side again. I was told to meet him in the garden when the church bells rang Vespers. Assuming I was going to have to demonstrate to him how well I'd learned from Father Julian, I first changed into clean clothes and scrubbed carefully in the basin. Then, exactly at Vespers, I strode confidently into the garden.

The Bishop was already there in a dark recess, sitting casually on a bench. His legs were crossed at the ankles, stretched out before him, and his hands were folded as if in prayer in his lap. "You have not learned a silent approach, Malcolm," he said with a smile and looked up. "I heard you from the moment you entered the garden."

"I'm sorry, your Eminence, I did not realize that you required stealth." I stood before him.

"I don't, but you should learn that it is a quality that often heightens arousal." He did not offer his ring for kissing. Instead, he leaned back, supporting himself on his arms.

I recognized the posture as an invitation, so I knelt down, unfolded his legs, and placed one hand under his cassock. "Your skin is warm and welcoming on this chilly evening," I said, looking into his eyes.

"Don't rush," he whispered, "Savor."

I did as the bishop commanded, dallying to take my pleasure and to give him the same. The church bells finally rang Compline, which I took as our signal to end. I helped him to button his cassock and readjust his *zuchetto* which had fallen askew on his head. I kissed each of his hands. "You have honored me, your Eminence."

"The formality excites me anew, Malcolm, but please, sit here next to me and hear me out." He patted the space beside him.

I sat down but kept hold of one of his hands. I was flushed with pride: I had satisfied him and myself not only sexually but emotionally. I felt a kinship with him, even as I understood that we were not equals – would never be – but related to one another. For a brief moment, I wondered if this was how a father and son loved one another.

"You have been with me for half a year. I hope you have learned what I sought to teach you."

"Of course. And I am very grateful, Bishop." I kissed his knuckles and put my other hand on his knee.

"What I do, what I have had you learn, these are ideas and actions older than Mother Church, Malcolm." He pressed his hand on mine. "Our couplings, with whatever gender, are celebrations of the rise of Dionysus – also called Zagreus or Liber – from the dead after those who were jealous of his free spirit tore him to pieces. His heart was saved from destruction in order for the gods to reconstruct him once again."

I barely understood what the bishop was saying. "Are these other names for God?"

"Not the Christian God, no, Malcolm. He rises to lead us to a heavenly reward. Dionysus, on the other hand, rises to lead us to our earthly reward of unmitigated pleasure. Have you not enjoyed it?"

"Most certainly. It has made me forget these physical weaknesses that have kept me an outsider all my life."

"Oh, no, Malcolm, you must not! These have been the marks, the signs, for me that you were meant to join me in this secret worship. I had only to wait for your ignorant grandfather to release you to me." At that, the Bishop lifted my eyepatch and kissed my hidden eye. "Hide this from me no longer; it is my beacon to pleasure."

"So, are we to have each other like this forever?" I asked, thrilling with the thought that I had finally found my safe haven.

"No, Malcolm. Our brief assignation tonight is my farewell to you, at least for some years. You must carry forth our Dionysian faith with discretion. I am sending you tomorrow to a monastery not far from here where you will study for the priesthood. Your body has learned its pleasures well; it's time to do the same for your mind. When I see you again, it will be to ordain you at last, my son." He pressed a rough coin into my palm and kissed my lips fervently.

In my room, my meager possessions tied in a bundle, I looked at the coin. It was more like a nugget than a smooth coin, bearing the silhouette of a man's face with a forked beard and a wreath on his head. All the carved lettering had worn away except for the word DIONYSUS. I fell asleep with the coin held firmly in my hand, next to the pearl that Grandfather said belonged to my mother.

The next day, I was placed in a cart with my belongings and driven to a boat that took me to the eponymous Abbey on the isle of Inchcolm. It had begun as a priory for Augustinians but was made into a full Abbey about thirty years before I was born. In many respects, it was a place still attempting to establish its character, so I did not feel the weight of tradition being imposed on me. I accepted my novitiate with aplomb and kept the Dionysian coin on my person at all times.

Abbey Life

The Abbey, being relatively new, was underdeveloped. Its living quarters and common areas were established because the Augustinians had had its priory here. However,

the chapel and other buildings were still being furnished to serve the monastic congregation of fifty men.

I arrived with a letter from Bishop Joseph to the Abbot. Brice was elderly and frail. He greeted me with disinterest, which I immediately interpreted as boredom with his position. I suspected that he wanted only to be given a warm, dark corner where he could sleep away his last days. "So, Bishop Joseph sends you?" he asked, holding the sealed letter in his hand.

"Yes, sir." I was clutching my bundle of possessions.

"Address me as 'Dom Brice', please. I prefer the simple and humble, as is the wont of we Augustinian Canons."

"Yes, Dom Brice," I muttered. "May I sit?" I indicated the stool beside me.

"No need. I'll read the bishop's missive later and then discuss with you your regimen here. Meanwhile," he rang a tiny handbell on his desk, "Brother William will show you your bed."

I nodded, and Brother William, who I suspected had been lurking just outside the office, appeared and said, "I'll take care of him, Dom. This way, please."

As we walked, Brother William pointed out the various parts of the monastery: the refectory containing two long rough-hewn tables where we took our meals, the calefactory where the huge fireplace crackled with a midsize fire this autumn day, the cloisters with its many bookcases and desks, and the chapter house filled with prie-dieus, off of which was a single large room with rows of single beds. "This is our dormitory. Your bed will be next to mine, here," he pointed at the first two beds in the room, "until you are more familiar with the abbey. Then, we'll move you farther inside, where you'll enjoy more privacy." William smiled thinly. "Such as it is."

Indeed, I thought there was no privacy in such an arrangement. I had slept cozily with my mother for most of my life. Then, at the bishop's, I enjoyed – for the first time – a room of my own, a condition I easily became accustomed to. Now, I'm thrown into a cavernous room filled with strangers. Inside, I despaired of any delight, but outwardly, remembering the bishop's admonitions to appear obedient, I smiled and nodded. "Thank you, Brother William."

"Put your possessions under the bed." Pulling a neatly folded garment from a shelf in the wall, he said, "Here, you will wear the Canon Regular." He shook out a black, floor-length tunic and held up a black leather belt. "Dom Brice will award you your hood after you get your tonsure, probably in a day or two."

I took the robe and belt. "Tonsure?" I asked.

William pointed to his own head. "We shave our heads, leaving only a fringe of hair to show our humility and devotion."

I blanched. I felt neither humility nor devotion; the bishop had secretly taught me exactly the opposite. "Required, I suppose?"

William looked at me quizzically. "Expected."

He was showing me the cloister library when another monk appeared to say that Dom Brice required my presence. I'd already changed into the tunic, although I still stood out as a stranger because of my shoes – the monks wore sandals – and my unshaven head. William pointed me in the direction of the abbot's office and said, "Come back here when he dismisses you."

My second audience with Dom Brice was somewhat warmer. He actually stood up when I entered his office, and then helped me to sit on the stool.

"You look like you are taking to monastic life quite adequately," he said, pointing to my tunic. "I'll have William bring you some sturdy sandals tonight." He nodded, pleased, then sat again at his desk.

"I understand I'm to lose most of my hair," I said, unable

to keep the anxiety out of my voice.

"Ah, but I'll give you a hood immediately after, which, if you choose, you can wear everywhere in the monastery except in the chapel. And, to honor the bishop's request, I'm allowing you to keep your eyepatch."

I touched the patch, suddenly self-conscious. "I was not aware it needed special dispensation."

"All of us wear the same attire, no? We show humility and willingly surrender our individual selves to communal grace. The eyepatch is a distraction, yes?"

"The purpose of the patch was to dispel the distraction of the sight underneath," I answered defensively.

"Let's see it, then," Brice challenged.

I lifted the patch gingerly and jutted my head forward for the abbot to have a clear look.

He stared deeply at me. Looked at the eye, then my face, then back at the eye. "Cover it if you wish," he said, sitting back, "but I personally think that when such evil is exposed to the light of day, its power fades with each rising of the sun."

I made a pitch for sympathy. "All my life, this eye has made me an outcast and kept me from participating in normal human society. The patch has given me relief from such a state."

"Hiding our sins is just another sin itself," Brice responded. "But the bishop has indicated in his letter that many blessings, both spiritual and material, will come to the abbey if we just concede to his specific wishes in regard to you. Apparently, he holds you dear and expects great things from you."

"He has been my most generous benefactor," I answered, bowing my head. "I have promised him that I would study with the greatest attention if it pleases him."

"Yes, yes. He has specifically asked that you be taught whatever knowledge of the ancients has been passed down to us. Thus, you will embark on Latin immediately and reading and writing, of course. Within the year, you will also learn

Greek; you are fortunate that we have language scholars among our ranks. You will work exclusively with our extensive text collection."

"I had heard that monks were usually engaged in manual labor, Dom," I said.

"We are Augustinians. We prize scholarship more and leave the field labors to the Benedictines and the Cistercians. Lay brothers do our everyday tasks; we mostly toil in the library."

I smiled broadly. "Indeed, I am enthusiastic about embarking on my studies."

That night, I was issued a second tunic and told that for hygienic purposes, one was for wearing and the other for sleeping. At the bells of Compline, William, from his bed near me, asked, "Do you have any questions, Malcolm?"

"No, William. I only wish the bed had more straw and the blanket were a bit thicker." I snickered in the dark.

William got up and lay down next to me. "I will warm you until you fall asleep," he said, cuddling close to me. "Unless you object, of course."

The heat of his body both relaxed and aroused me. "I am glad of it," I assured him.

"Stay still. I do this only to welcome and comfort you, Malcolm, nothing more. I understand that celibacy is more difficult for some than for others. You will find, once your bed is moved farther back into the shadows of the dormitory, that others are willing to engage in a more robust comfort; you must decide whether or not to accept their advances. But, whatever you do, please keep your judgments to yourself. Revealing the preferences of others does no good, and it only disrupts the serenity of cloistered life. Do you understand?"

"With joy, yes." The discretion at the monastery relieved me.

"Now, before you sleep, show me your eye that I may kiss

it, for I derive pleasure from discovering deformities in others. It is my one small vice."

I pulled off the patch, thus allowing William to lay with his lips on my eye while I fell asleep. When I was awakened at 4 a.m. for meditative prayer, William was already kneeling at his bedside, and my patch lay untied on my pillow.

I was tonsured and given a grey hood to indicate that I was a novice and would receive a black hood to match my robe only after I'd proven myself worthy. Under the direction of William and those monks who were the most versed in ancient texts, I progressed quickly as a student of classical studies at Abbey Inchcolm. Halfway to age sixteen, I had earned my black hood.

I could read and write English and Latin and enjoyed reading, if haltingly, in Greek. Many manuscripts passed through Inchcolm, for it was part of a chain of monasteries throughout the British Isles and the western Continent that shared whatever papers were brought by pilgrims returning from the Holy Land. Once a monastery had copied a manuscript, sometimes taking close to a year, it was passed along to another monastery where it could also be copied. Thus was knowledge disseminated, slowly but surely, and sometimes inaccurately, throughout the civilized world. I felt like I had all of mankind's wisdom at my disposal.

The more I read and learned, the more I understood myself to be above and beyond others. I had left behind the gutter boy reviled by everyone, the cripple, evil-eyed one who earned only scorn. The ordinary men in the monastery – those most devout and zealous about their religious calling – made a wide path around me; they were the same as those petty people I'd left behind in Inverkeithing. I was glad for their avoidance, for it meant that I need not deal with them nor explain myself or my actions to them.

There were others, however, the ones I called "like-minded," who shared either (sometimes both!) my thirst for knowledge and my sexual proclivities. Ah, yes, as to the latter.

Brother William had quite courteously pointed out that monastic silence sometimes means simply minding one's own business. So, once I discovered among the monks, but especially among the lay brothers who worked with their hands, some men who were unafraid and even eager for sexual adventures, I continued my lustful pursuits discreetly but without restraint. My Dionysian coin, lying hidden in my robe, shone brightly each time I rubbed its surface in pursuit of or in completion of a sexual encounter. The only thing I missed was the presence of women in this cloistered environment. And for that longing, I rubbed my pearl; it reminded me of a woman's smooth skin.

One day, a Scottish pilgrim from Crete brought a sheaf of papers which he'd obtained from some peasants who lived at the foot of Mount Ida; he'd exchanged a box of spices for the manuscripts and, not able to read Greek, could not ascertain the value of the papers. However, being an old friend of Dom Brice, he donated the papers to Inchcolm, hoping only for the abbot's blessing in return.

The brother who had taught me Greek, Brother Alfred, was old, his eyesight failing exactly as his father's had: it started with a loss of night vision, then peripheral vision. Eventually, he could not distinguish the close penmanship of ancient manuscripts. As a result, I, alone, of all the brothers, was called upon to read any Greek texts that we acquired.

The boxful of scrolls and loose pages from Crete were delicate; they'd been kept in an unsealed wooden crate overlaid with dust and moisture. I had to handle them most gently, as I would a virgin I was about to ravage. I realized that my intellectual curiosity had developed so acutely that it aroused my sexual nature as well. I chuckled at the irony.

Left to discover and evaluate the papers by myself, I learned what I came to believe was the true history of the legend of Zagreus. When I first came upon the name in the scrolls, I gasped. I'd heard the name only once, spoken by Bishop Joseph in his garden, when he pressed into my hand that gold coin, Dionysus. It was a portion of my life coming full circle.

My studies in Greek led me to conclude that the name Zagreus meant "hunter of game," for he was the god who hunted his prey at night and thereupon conducted feasts of raw flesh under torchlight. It was like a middle name attached to the given name Dionysus (so: "Dionysus Zagreus") for the child born of the union between Zeus, in the form of a serpent, and Persephone. He was brought, the scrolls said, to Mount Ida to be raised until Zeus declared him his heir as ruler of the universe.

But Hera jealously urged the Titans to kill the child. Distracting him with a mirror, they seized him and tore him to pieces. Then, they boiled, roasted, and partially ate the pieces. Only Athena, the goddess of wisdom and war, saved his heart from which Zeus was able to perform Dionysus' reincarnation.

I realized that Athena, associated with intellect, saved her half-brother Dionysus Zagreus, associated with ecstasy and insanity, as if the two opposites, although in perpetual conflict, needed one another to survive. I whispered to myself that night, "Without evil, good does not exist." And I masturbated.

Ordination

My discovery of the story about Dionysus Zagreus whetted my appetite for more information about this god and the rituals surrounding him. Bishop Joseph had intimated that Dionysus was the god we should be most devoted to, but he provided no other information. These recently gained papers told of the god's origins but not much more. Now that I had learned to read and write with some fluency, I wanted more, exactly the way my sexual appetites had grown from curiosity to hungry experience.

I scoured the Inchcolm library for more information on Dionysus and Zagreus, but I came up empty-handed. My purpose was to discover ways in which I could expand my devotion to Dionysus in order to win that god's favor, although I had no idea of the benefits that might be bestowed on me. However, I was soon to discover that I might need some Dionysian intercession. On my seventeenth birthday, I was summoned to Dom Brice's office.

"Did you know that Bishop Joseph and I have corresponded about you on a regular basis?" Brice looked more ancient to me with each passing year. I was frankly surprised that he had not chosen to withdraw from his position and appoint William his successor.

"No, Dom. However, might I inquire as to the Bishop's well-being? He is very dear to me." I had not seen Bishop Joseph for a long time, during which I'd matured considerably.

"You've studied here for more than two years, Malcolm."

"Yes, Dom. I have learned a great deal. I might even say that I've become quite scholarly."

Brice shook his head. "There is the one way you haven't changed much. You are still quite prideful, Malcolm, despite our numerous examples of humility here at Inchcolm."

I bowed my head, hoping I looked ashamed, although I didn't feel so at all. "I'm sorry, Dom. Clearly, I still have much to learn." *But it won't be at your hands,* I thought.

"The Bishop has written, asking when you will be ordained into the priesthood, Malcolm. Frankly, I thought you would prefer to remain in the monastic brotherhood, continuing with your studies in texts and bringing honor to the monastery's studies."

I tried to gauge Brice's openness to my ordination; he seemed unenthusiastic, or perhaps he was already bemoaning the end of the bishop's contributions. "Oh, Dom, of course, I would prefer the monastic life of withdrawal, but I must give myself to the wishes of the Bishop, of course, as one of his ecclesiastical subjects." I clasped my hands in prayer and hid my face; I was finding it difficult not to smile at my clever deception.

"Of course, of course," Brice said, clearly disappointed. "So also must I obey the Bishop. Therefore, let's set your ordination for six months from now. I'll assign William to immediately begin your priestly training – administering all the sacraments and Mass, ministering to a parish, and so forth. It will be quite different from monastic life."

"I will do my best to adjust and to learn with my utmost ability." The world! I thought. I was going to go back to the world!

"I must tell you, Malcolm, that, truthfully, I will not be sorry to see you go. You must understand that I say this without malice but with a hope that you will see your shortcomings and correct them as best you can."

"Of course, Dom Brice. I would be grateful for your opinion." I smiled sweetly.

"Your time here has been both good and bad. First, the good: these are observations on which you can take comfort. When you are interested in something, you have no boundaries or limits. It is an unusual and enviable enthusiasm. You have incredible mental skills: you learn quickly, you adapt to circumstances easily, and you are generous to share what you've learned. And, of course, the bishop's generosity cannot be ignored."

Ignoring the reference to the bishop, I said, "I was brought up a lonely child. I feel I have flourished here in the company of men."

"Ah, and then there are your shortcomings, Malcolm. Please take this as a lesson for improvement. You are, as I've said, prideful, slow to see others as your betters or even as your equal. You refuse to see your good qualities as gifts from God for which you should be grateful, while you insist that some of your failings, particularly your physical disabilities of leg and eye, are only the cruel mistakes of God (as if He could make mistakes!), rather than signs that should lead you to atonement. I have watched you closely, Malcolm, and you seem not to yearn for God's grace." Brice shook his head.

"I say this with humility: you misjudge me, Dom Brice. You are not the first, nor will you be the last. But, mark this: I will prove myself the better person worthy of Paradise by my wit and my actions." I cared nothing for Brice's criticism of me; I was thinking of how, as a priest, I would be freed from the confines of this monastery, how I would have greater access to the larger world of knowledge and experience. My liberation was at hand! *My* paradise was not that insipid place of angels groveling before God.

The six months of preparation passed quickly and uneventfully. The best part of this time was that I was allowed to let my tonsure grow out, ridding me of that stupid bald spot. William attended to my education thoroughly, allowing me little time for studies other than those related to becoming a priest.

"You are ruthless, William," I said one day after he made me repeat from memory the Latin prayer for administering Extreme Unction. "This is probably the thirtieth time you've made me say the damned words."

"The way you keep making errors in the prayer does, in fact, make it damned," he responded. "You'll never send any poor dead soul to heaven if you don't give it clear directions." He snickered at his own mocking of my shortcomings. "Again, Malcolm."

"Per istam sanctam Unctionem et suam piisimam misericordiam, indulgeat tibi Dominus quidquid per sensum deliquisti," I said slowly and deliberately.

"Huzzah, Malcolm, finally!" William clapped me on my back.

I smiled. We were sitting in the last row of the chapel pews, so I reached back and dunked my fingers in the holy water fount. Playfully flicking the water at William, I repeated the prayer in English: "Through this holy anointing and God's holy mercy, may the Lord forgive you whatever sins you committed through your senses."

"This means you're ready, Malcolm, for your ordination." William dabbed at the water on his face and turned serious. "It means a complete change for you, Malcolm. To be ordained is to be marked indelibly with special grace."

"Why had you never gone on to be ordained, William?"

"Has no one ever told you my story?" William turned around to scan the chapel as if making sure we were alone.

"No. Few here talk to me. Even fewer would share rumors or gossip with me. I am not liked."

"You are not trusted, Malcolm. It isn't a question of like-ability. The men here sense your aloofness and self-confidence. You have not sought their trust, and they wouldn't confide in you. Yet, my story isn't well-known."

"Then, out with it, man! I am to become a priest. Perhaps one day I will administer Extreme Unction to you, so I should know what you need to be forgiven for, eh?"

William nodded thoughtfully. "I took Holy Orders as a convenience rather than as a vocation."

"That's nothing new, William. Most here have probably done the same. Monasteries are, I think, largely filled with men who have no skills with which to succeed in the outside world."

"Not a lack of skills, Malcolm." William bowed his head. "I had very well-developed skills indeed. I was a master thief, a criminal of the basest sort, and ultimately a murderer." When I said nothing, he went on. "I did not murder in self-defense. It was not during a robbery. I wasn't drunk or deceived or betrayed. It was an act of love, but murder nonetheless."

I found William's story fascinating and exciting. I covered my mouth with my hand to hide the fact that I was licking my lips in delicious anticipation of hearing more.

William searched my face for a reaction. Finding none, he continued. "My mother was sick, very sick. She begged me to release her from her pain, so I strangled her. As my hands tightened around her throat, I watched her eyes. At first, they seemed to find peace. But then, as her body sought breath, her eyes turned dark with panic. She struggled against me as if to rescind her request for release. But I liked it. I held her down until her life was gone, until her body went limp."

"You fulfilled her last request, William. That's all."

"No, I had spent my whole life stealing from people. This was the ultimate theft, and it thrilled me. I stole her life. And I enjoyed it. With that knowledge, I fled to the monastery and made up a story about having a vision of being called to religious service. So you find me here."

"But surely, William, your life here has been atonement for that act." I realized that I was not sincere; I was simply mouthing what I thought I should say as an ordained priest.

"You've not heard the worst. I remain here in monastic life as a success: I am admired by my fellow monks, I am indispensable to the abbot for my skills, and all of this is simply a small part of the greater pride I feel – that I have succeeded in escaping punishment for my crime, that I have successfully hidden away here undiscovered. I'm not atoning, Malcolm, I'm gloating."

"No one is without sin, William." I stood up, held his head in my heads, kissed his forehead, then his lips. "No one."

My ordination was a quiet and private affair. The day after my eighteenth birthday, Bishop Joseph celebrated Mass at the Abbey, accompanied by his subaltern Father Julian. The night before, the two of them visited me in my room. The bishop had aged badly in my eyes: his sallow skin hung loosely on his frame, and he emitted a slightly repulsive odor as if his body were already decaying. I was relieved that he had become a mere voyeur, wanting only to watch while Julian and I satisfied one another. After we finished, Bishop Joseph insisted that each of us kiss his ring. It took all my effort not to visibly gag at his smell.

At the close of the Mass the next morning, the winter sun streaming in through the narrow chapel windows, Joseph called me forward. Dressed in white, I knelt then lay supine before the bishop while all the monks knelt in place.

Joseph, seated in front of the altar, leaned down and laid his hand on my head. "May the Holy Spirit fill you with the power of God's grace," he said.

This was the signal for the congregation to recite the Litany of the Saints, starting with "Lord, have mercy on us, Christ have mercy on us. . ." and continuing for the next fifteen minutes with beseeching all the denizens of heaven to bless us.

My body laid against the floor, my forehead and nose pressed into those stones. I kept telling myself that this discomfort was worth the reward of ordination. I hated the ritual, however: the droning, monotonous prayers, the sticky scent of the incense, the cold air, the sliver of sunshine sliding downward as the hours passed.

Finally, the bishop's hand pressed heavily as he said, "Malcolm, you are now a minister of Words and Sacrament in the church of Jesus Christ. Be faithful and true in your ministry so that your whole life will bear witness to the crucified and risen Christ."

I murmured, "Amen," and started to rise.

Just then, the entire congregation was startled by the harsh, rattling call of a magpie at the window. Someone called out, "Devil, devil, I defy thee!" and with clacking wings, the magpie flew off.

Joseph offered his hand to help me up and rose himself. As we both straightened up, he pulled me to him and whispered in my ear, "I have arranged your parish to be your old home, Inverkeithing. Go there presently and proclaim your prize. We shall not meet again, my son." The next day, Bishop Joseph was gone back to Edinburgh.

Father Julian stayed on to manage the details of my departure from Inchcolm and to give me instructions regarding my installation as the new parish priest of St. Peter's in Inverkeithing. "Here are some vestments that the bishop has left for you. Leave behind the rags you've been wearing here at the monastery." He handed me a large parcel containing two sets of garments required for celebrating Mass and assorted casual attire like cassocks. "And here's a bit to get you started in the parish – you'll need to have shoes, belts, and a new eyepatch made and find a woman to do your laundry and cook your meals." He handed me a small purse of coins. "And this," he said, handing me something wrapped in soft cloth.

It was a gold chalice, thin at the cup part but heavy at the pommel. "A chalice?"

"It is customary for the family to give one of these when the boy is ordained," Julian said. "This is quite valuable; take care of it."

"Why did the bishop say we wouldn't meet again?"

"Because he's done with you. He'll be looking for fresh, younger meat if you know what I mean."

"Another son?" I would not betray the relief I felt at this news; the bishop's odor disgusted me.

"So to speak," Julian said, laughing. "And, by the way, he insists that you take the name 'John' once you install yourself as parish priest. The bishop says that you need to forget your ties to the Murray family now. You're *tabula rasa*; make the most of it."

I frowned, uncertain if I was being set free or being dismissed. "I won't forget you, Julian," I said sincerely.

"Better that you do. I'm leaving now. I've arranged for a carriage to take you to Inverkeithing in the morning, John." He turned and left.

It was mid-morning when the carriage dropped me off at St. Peter's in Chains. The driver, having noticed my eye patch and my limp when he picked me up, had asked, "Was you at Ronaldsway?" He was referring to a 1275 uprising on the Isle of Man by Manx rebels attempting to reinstall the Norse dynasty; the rebels were crushed by the Scottish army.

"I was just thirteen," I answered evasively.

"It's the young ones who get hurt the most when men fight," the driver commented. Then, nodding at my clerical collar, he added, "I think God tested you and rewarded you with your collar." He smiled approvingly.

"Perhaps so." I closed my eyes to indicate that I wished no further conversation.

When he dropped me off, placing my parcels on the ground beside me, he asked, "Would you bless me, Father?" and genuflected before me.

My first act as a priest! I was delighted and put my hand on the man's head. "*Spiritus sapientie informet cogitationes tuas.* May the spirit of wisdom inform your thoughts."

"Amen," he murmured.

I took out the small purse of coins.

"No, sir, your blessing is payment enough," he said, getting back in his carriage. "I was told to wait for another who is expected in Edinburgh today."

Before I could ask, the old Father Philip appeared, carrying a stout leather bag. "So, the prodigal son returns," he said sourly. "I should have known I wouldna be rid of Malcolm Murray so easily."

I looked at him with pretended surprise. "I am Father John, pleased to meet you." I put my hand on his shoulder.

"John?" he sneered.

I pressed my fingers into his shoulder until he winced a bit. "Yes, as required by Rome, although I prefer Ian." I added, "I understand that Bishop Joseph is expecting you, sir. It is from his eminence that we both take our instructions, isn't that so?"

"Uh, yes." Philip peered at me. "But I will forever know yer by yer true name."

I steered him into the carriage. "The Bishop is not known for his patience, sir." And, clearly perplexed, he was gone.

"My parish!" I said aloud, looking at the stoneworks of the Church. Local legend reported that St. Erat, a holy man who followed St. Ninian, worshipped here, but when I researched both names at Inchcolm, there was nothing but speculation. The early Church had bestowed sainthood on them, but they were unremarkable to successive generations; I understood this to be my opportunity to overlay onto the scant stories of St. Erat my own interpretations and imaginings.

My integration with the people of Inverkeithing went awkwardly but swiftly. No one missed the mean-spirited Father Philip, and most had never met that bastard boy Malcolm of the Murray family; I was simply Father John, regrettably maimed in the Battle of Ronaldsway. When I enquired about the Murray family, I was told that only the old man survived; his wife had died peacefully in her sleep, and his mad daughter, having heard that her child had disappeared, drowned herself in the bay. I told my congregation to pray for them.

I acted the part of parish priest brilliantly. I performed all the sacraments awarded to priests: the celebration of Mass, hearing confession and giving absolution, Baptism, Matrimony, and Extreme Unction. I indulged my personal desires discreetly. For example, I found through confession those who wanted the same pleasures as I wanted. In addition, I convinced those ignorant peasants that, as the priest officiating, I had the right of *prima nocta*, that is, to bed the bride on her wedding night. I explained to those who hesitated that it was a ritual to cleanse the virgins for matrimony. In short, I had found my safe haven.

My Dionysus studies were considerably curtailed here at Inverkeithing, where there was no library and no pilgrims appearing with manuscripts and scrolls from the Eastern edges of the world. I wrote to Inchcolm where pitying me, Brother William gathered some duplicate materials and sent them to me so that I could remain fluent in Latin and Greek. And, one day, he prepared a surprise for me.

I'd been at St. Peter's for a full year when a stranger arrived on horseback at the Church gates. Dusty from the road but clearly a nobleman, he said he had a message for me from Brother William. I offered him supper and a place to sleep overnight before he left for Edinburgh.

"You are Father John, once the monk called Malcolm?" he inquired before accepting my invitation.

"Yes, the same. There is a story behind the name change but, I think, not pertinent." I led him to my table. "I'll inform Rosie to cook a supper for two. I can also give you some whiskey or wine if you prefer."

"I've been in Scotland for weeks now, and I've developed a taste for your whiskey, thank you."

"Where have you come from?"

"Most recently, from Brother William, who referred you to me, or me to you, as it were. He oversees the monastery's library." He sipped at the whiskey I put before him. "My name is Sir Hubert von Walt. I've been a crusader, but with the fall of Constantinople, am a mercenary to any who can pay my fee."

"I'm sure that William could not afford you. I hope you realize that I, too, would be unable to meet your monetary requirement."

"I brought him some manuscripts that I'd acquired in my travels, and I was not asking much for them. Since I do not know Greek, I did not understand the contents. William, however, thought that this one might be of interest to you. He insisted to me that it had no value beyond your scholarly interest and that you could pay me fairly for it."

"Why not find a wealthier buyer? I am, as you see, a mere parish priest."

"I have other – uh, artifacts that some would pay more for. Objects, I mean, not mere scrolls. I'd hoped that you, like William, would grant me some blessing for this service, in addition to the nominal fee, of course."

"After supper, will you allow me to examine this manuscript so I might ascertain its value to me?"

"Most assuredly, Father John. Could I trouble you for more whiskey, however?"

By candlelight, Hubert and I carefully unwrapped the vellum pages of the manuscript. "Where did you acquire this?" It smelled vaguely of seawater and olive oil.

"Escaping from Constantinople, I crossed the Propontis and spent time in Bursa, a city rich with silk. There, I found my military skills useful to the wealthy traders. This particular manuscript, however, came from a harem girl who gave me this to help her escape the harem."

"This, and what else?" I asked. I knew that Hubert would not risk his life for a manuscript.

Hubert blushed. "Some marvelous and unforgettable nights. Unlike me," he said, smiling, "she thought the sheaf of papers more valuable than herself."

When I did a cursory examination of the manuscript, I noted references to Brumalia which, I knew from previous studies, was a pagan festival that had been forbidden by the Church as early as the seventh century. I wanted to study this manuscript more closely. "So, what would you want for this?"

"Not your worthless Scottish coin, I'll say. An object of value, perhaps?"

I had only three items of value to anyone: the pearl that Grandfather had pressed into my hand, the Dionysian coin that Bishop Joseph had given me, and the gold chalice I'd been awarded at my ordination. The pearl and coin were always with me, safe in a small pouch I wore around my neck. The chalice was hidden in my chambers. "The chalice in the cabinet on the altar in St. Peter's is silver. Would that be adequate?" It was the chalice used for Mass, blessed and allocated to the church when it was consecrated.

He hesitated.

"I also have this pearl." I pulled it from my pouch and let it roll across the table to him. "It is a personal memento from family."

"Along with your blessing and a written pardon, I would accept these as payment." Hubert bowed his head and smiled.

"Done." In fact, I was glad to be free of my last connection to the Murray family.

After Hubert left Inverkeithing, I complained to my congregation that he had been a scoundrel who had taken advantage of my Christian charity by stealing, in the dark of the night, the chalice from the unlocked church. They were angry and desolate; how was I to celebrate the Eucharist without a chalice?

"I was given a wondrous chalice for my ordination by Bishop Joseph," I explained, "which I offer as a substitute for the stolen one."

They sighed and gasped. They protested that it was too dear an item for their poor church. Eventually, however, they conceded to my suggestion, which made it easier for me to have their acquiescence in whatever I required.

The manuscript was a revelation to me. It described in minute detail the celebration of Brumalia, a mid-winter pagan feast in honor of wine-making. Popular in rural areas, the Brumalia included women dancing in public, and participants wearing Dionysian masks and invoking Bacchus' benediction. I had experienced orgies, but only within the confines of private residences where participants had been carefully chosen. They were discreet. Brumalia was public, a novelty to me. In fact, it began to dominate my thoughts.

A year of parish life, no matter how much I bent it to my own purposes, was beginning to bore me. When I was first informed that I'd be leaving Inchcolm, I believed it was my liberation from a stultifying existence. I felt the monastery to be no more than my prison, a place where I'd been locked away from the variety of life.

Yet, there was the library. It saved me from utter oblivion. There were so many scrolls and manuscripts to read, so many worthy of copying despite the labor involved in such a task. The library was a constant source of discovery for me: reading the ideas of wise men, the wild tales of adventurers, and the fervent prayers of holy men. I could not help but be enthralled by such company.

But, back to Inverkeithing. It amused me for a time. Then, as all of its existence was manipulated by my will, the town seemed less a conquest to me than a deadly routine. Save for a few of the skeptical town elders, I could persuade or compel the natives to believe any story I might fashion, or to do whatever I bade in the name of God. Once, this influence was a delicious and satisfying game; it had become tiresome in how easily I could effect it.

So, Brumalia began to represent to me a new way to demonstrate my power over others. It was particularly attractive not only for its public nature but also because it required people to engage in activities they would otherwise consider inappropriate. "I can make them do anything," I whispered to myself as I planned the activity. I could make Inverkeithing famous; more, I could gain favor with Dionysus.

Brumalia

Brumalia was a pagan ritual performed during the winter solstice, essentially a recognition of seasonal change: the days became shorter and the nights longer. However, it was early March now – Spring soon to begin – and I had no wish to wait until November or December to mount a celebration. So, I chose Easter as my target date. I had only to draw some parishioners into the plan.

First, the young people. During Bible studies classes, I drew aside three of them who I thought I could most easily persuade. "Easter will soon be upon us," I said, "but do any of you know about Brumalia?"

The three shook their heads and shrugged uneasily.

"It was started by the first Roman Christians who had to celebrate it in hiding else they would be persecuted by the Romans who worshipped Jupiter."

Mark, a young man of thirteen, asked, "Is it a saint's day?"

"No, a celebration of Christ the Eucharist," I lied in explanation.

"Why have we never heard of it?" asked Julia, a sweet eleven-year-old with bright red hair and a freckled face.

"It is special, meant only for the most devout to celebrate," I intoned. After a pause, I added, "Not unlike the three of you who I have noticed are so eager at prayers."

They blushed, especially Emma, the same age as Mark. Her light brown hair sparkled with strands of blonde in the sunlight, and her complexion was pale like the color of wheat fields just sprouting in March.

One time, a month earlier, I had drawn Mark and Emma into an embrace as a way of expressing my satisfaction with them for completing a task I'd set them on. I held each by the waist and could feel the heat rising from their innocent flesh. I wanted not to initiate them myself into the joys of sexual pleasures; I wanted them to despoil each other, taking my pleasure in the fact that I introduced them.

"I was thinking that perhaps," I started, carefully watching their faces for interest, "we could initiate our own Brumalia celebration here at St. Peter's."

"We'd be happy to help, Father," Emma volunteered. "Right?" She looked at her two companions.

"Of course!" Mark readily agreed.

"In secret?" Julia asked apprehensively. She had been taught that secrets were vehicles for deceit.

"No," I assured her. "We would share it widely, hoping to convince others to join us."

Julia nodded but was still mulling over the information. The two others nodded with much more enthusiasm. "Tell us about it, would you?" They were of an age that sought out delight and pleasure.

I smiled. I had already carefully planned my description. "It is a kind of re-enactment or what we could call an interpretation of the Eucharist as described in John 6, which says *Whoever eats my flesh and drinks my blood has eternal life. Whoever eats my flesh and drinks my blood remains in me, and I in him.* You remember that, don't you?"

"Yes, Father. You told us it was something called trans— trans—" Julia hesitated.

"Transubstantiation," offered Mark.

"Yes, exactly." I squeezed Mark's shoulder. "It applies to the bread and wine at Mass, which we know is miraculously turned into Christ's body and blood. But during Brumalia, we demonstrate the eating and drinking in symbolic ways."

"I don't understand," Emma said.

"The ritual remains private, but its proclamation shall be public and joyful – a display of its successful completion. I must instruct you about the ritual itself, and you, in turn, must find others to join you in its completion; then, all of us shall celebrate it publicly. In fact," I said, "I already have the names of some who might be willing to participate without too much convincing."

"I'm excited to learn," Mark said, hunching forward.

"Julia," I said, taking the girl's small, soft hand, "because you are the youngest, I will myself help you to observe the ritual and teach it to others. For now, I'm afraid you must leave me with Mark and Emma alone." The latter two smiled, but Julia frowned.

"Why?"

"You'll understand when it comes your turn, sweet child," I said, pointing her to the door. "Tomorrow, the latest." When she was gone, those of us remaining chuckled at her obvious despondency. I locked the door, explaining that I wanted to insure our privacy.

It was a simple thing to introduce Mark and Emma to the sexual intimacies they might now freely enjoy with my blessing. As expected, they were shy at first, but with my encouragement and assurances that they would feel quite marvelous, they did as I directed, step by lusty step. At the conclusion of their first sexual intercourse (and some accompanying extras to which I introduced them), their shyness returned until I explained to them how much pleasure they had also afforded me in observing them. So eager to please, they were delighted that this new activity provided me with some measure of satisfaction as well. I told them they must go home and secretly practice and, in a week or so, return to demonstrate to me how much they'd improved. At that time, as well, I would reveal the nature of our public proclamation of Brumalia.

The next day, I initiated Julia myself, knowing that she would more readily accept the caresses and embraces if I were the one giving them. I was very gentle with her, able to see when she was particularly fearful or pained. I was noble enough not to force her to intercourse, although I insisted – with great gentleness and sensitivity – that she submit to all other sexual acts. I was sure that repetitions of these activities would lead her eventually and naturally to finally submit to consummation. She would, I was certain, even desire it. Hours later, her tears dried, and she smiled bravely at me. When I touched her to test her reaction, she did not pull away but gasped quietly. It was my indication that I had awakened her appetite.

Two weeks later, a month before Easter, I met with the three again. Julia arrived first.

"I've done my tasks as you instructed, Father, touching and rubbing myself whenever I could find a private corner. I don't think I do this as well as you."

"We'll see," I said, sitting her on my lap and finding my way under her clothes. I ascertained with considerable objectivity that she was ready to complete her sexual education.

When Mark and Emma arrived, they basically presented a show for Julia and me of their licentiousness. They had no shame, no timidity. Their obvious enjoyment and unbounded energy excited me almost to distraction.

"Here is what we will do on Brumalia, which I decided will be on a most appropriate day, Holy Saturday, as a precursor to the celebrated Resurrection on Easter Sunday. We shall wear garlands and flowing robes. I shall lead the procession from the Church into the street and to the harbor, carrying a large image of Mark's ballocks before me, much like the holy crucifix we carry down the church aisles during High Mass. Mark shall follow solemnly but be continually touched and caressed by both Emma and Julia. Did any of you find others to join us?"

"Yes," Emma said immediately. Two of the young wives said you had lain with them on their marriage bed, Father, and they proclaimed the experience quite delightful. They wish to join."

"Some of the fellows said you engaged in lewd and suggestive conversations with them in the past," Mark added.

"When I asked if they might be interested in extending or expanding some of these ideas, they agreed to meet with me again to further our discussions."

"And I have also been busy," I added. "Five of the harlots and a few more of their regular customers have accepted my invitation to join us for a fee, of course. So, altogether, we seem to have about twenty in our parade. That number will encourage others along the route to the harbor to join in. There will be no controversy."

So we set about gathering our small but ostentatious party. On the day before, we found some amateur musicians at the pub to accompany us on flute, drum, and horn. Our actual procession through town was noisy and startling. Many simply stopped in their tracks and stared. Others leaned out of windows or lurked in doorways, watching with uncertain smiles. Children were hugged close but not prevented from observing. Some bystanders joined us, dancing lightly to the music and yelling encouragement to others to merge with us. Some even came out to offer us drinks and food.

Our parade was so unique, so unusual for Inverkeithing, that no one had the wit or time to protest it as untoward or even unholy. After all, I was the parish priest, the religious leader of this small town, and who would dare question why I was marching at the head of a parade holding aloft a four-foot plaster penis? Most spectators were amused, their laughter disguising their inability to make sense of the spectacle.

"Brumalia!" I shouted as I marched forward. "We celebrate the Holy body of Christ! We celebrate his power! Priapus!" I waved to everyone. "We celebrate the rebirth of the land! Join us!" Most were too ignorant to realize I was blending Christian and pagan mythology.

Mark walked beside me in thin garments I had designed to show the contours of his body. As the women in the parade — not only those who were part of the parade but some who joined spontaneously — pawed at him, hanging onto him or pressing themselves against him, Mark was clearly aroused, his mouth often twisting in a combination of pain and ecstasy.

Only when we arrived at the harbor, flushed with excitement and needing rest, did we see Grandfather Murray, who I'd not seen for years. He was stooped and wrinkled, leaning heavily on a stout carved staff. I looked forward to greeting him at last since he had not ever come to St. Peter's while I ministered there.

The procession broke up into small groups of people chattering contentedly, talking to those spectators who had followed our progression through the town. I saw some people whispering and embracing before they drifted off into side alleys or doorways. The air was a mixture of salty seawater and musk.

I was left standing alone, holding the large plaster penis aloft. I set it down and walked to Grandfather. "I think you might not recognize me, old man." I smiled broadly.

"They speak of yer as Father John, but I knew immediately that it was yer, Malcolm, who had come back – probably at that cursed bishop's insistence – to embarrass me and scorn the Murray name. I thought I was well rid of yer, but I see that I was mistaken."

"Grandfather, you are still my blood, your daughter, my beloved mother. Can we not make peace?" The Brumalia celebration had assured me that I was secure in my life at long last; this town was in my thrall.

"Yes, I will have peace," he said, suddenly removing a dirk from his waistband and stabbing me with surprising force in my heart.

I fell to the ground, the blood soaking my robe and bubbling up into my throat and onto my tongue. As my vision blurred, I saw a single magpie land heavily on a harbor pier. It did not take long for the darkness to slip over me, but I hoped that, like Dionysus, my followers, especially Julia and, Emma and Mark, would discover the miracle by which I could be reborn.

In that moment, that infinity of spirit, the essential ker-
nel of me, broke free and was grasped in the fist of Dionysus,
who hurled me forward in time to lodge fiercely in the soul of
yet another who disdained moderation to celebrate surfeit.

Manila Customs House (Alamy)

"A long and arduous journey," is what I answer when people ask me how was my trip from Sevilla to Veracruz. I do not add the other information that I hold within my memory: the food spoiled with worms and mold, the constant dampness of my robes, the monotonous days of endless horizons, the sleepless nights of water lapping against the sides of the ship, and the skittering rats' whiskers brushing my toes. I said a hundred words of thanks when we docked in that humid New Spain harbor filled with shouting sailors and the clanging metal armor and weapons of the conquistadors.

We survived with our Faith intact. It was almost mid-1562 when we landed after two and a half months at sea. We had heard just before we left Spain that war was brewing between the Spanish Hapsburgs in Holland and the Dutch who lived there and rejected being ruled by King Philip II because he favored the Spanish aristocracy. We heard of the Dutch rebels who declared themselves Calvinists, so we prayed that they would seek God's forgiveness before our zealous Catholic soldiers put them to the sword.

Our esteemed leader urged us to our knees even as we first set foot on land. "Pray, brothers, for all those we left behind in our beloved *España*, for *nuestro ejército* – our military – everywhere, and for *los paganos* – the pagans – whom we will bring to God's bosom."

We knelt there in our sweaty robes, smelling of ocean and vermin and filth, yet filled with the grace of our devotion to God, and I was sure that, despite all observations to the contrary, we glowed with the aura of God's blessing on us and our destiny to spread Catholicism as far and wide as possible. This harbor town, formally called Villa Rica de la Vera Cruz, was founded by the celebrated Hernán Cortés and his men some forty years earlier, declaring it a direct possession of the Spanish crown, thereby freeing it from the authority of the Governor of Cuba. Noted for its gold deposits and dedicated to the True Cross, it represented Spain's presence in the New World. For simplicity's sake, we Spaniards called this town Veracruz ('true cross'), the main entry point for immigrants to this land, New Spain.

We were greeted by a contingent of Franciscans, the first friars in New Spain, who showed us to our temporary quarters at their abbey. The accommodations were spare but welcome: clean and dry. Our dinner was a simple meal of chicken and what the Franciscans called *patatas*, a starchy, orange-colored boiled vegetable discovered in the fabled Andes Mountains of South America. The food was quite satisfying. And the Franciscans gladly shared with us the information we needed for our stay in Veracruz before we headed to our final destination, the Philippines.

"This town," explained Fray Francisco, "is the smaller version of all of New Spain." He was introduced to me as one of the first conquistadors to surrender his military life in favor of becoming a religious. He was a huge man, rough-hewn and robust, whose arms and hands rippled with muscles. He was at least fifteen years my senior, probably in his thirties.

"It is nothing like anything I have seen at home," I admitted.

"Veracruz is filled with immigrants from Spain – mostly soldiers and clergy – but is also home to African slaves and subjugated Aztec natives who we use for construction and other labor-intensive projects. The slaves have been brought from the nearby Caribbean islands, while the Aztec were the original pagan inhabitants who we conquered and converted. Many, however, fled into the surrounding jungles, places too thick and uncharted for us to venture into."

"How do all of you survive?" I asked.

"Trade, of course," Francisco explained. "This land is rich with silver, but also abundant with other goods prized by our brethren in Europe, such as red dye from insects, as well as chocolate, vanilla, and chili peppers. We are also a trading hub for fruits and sugar cane from the islands in the eastern sea called the Caribbean."

"So, you cultivate the land."

"No, we manage the cultivation. We are the nobility here, overseeing the work of the slaves and natives. After all, we have brought them the most precious gift of all: we have brought Christ into their hearts."

"But does that not mean that we teach them love?" I asked.

Francisco shook his head. "Sadly, too many resist us. So, we must continually remind them of our superiority in the hope that they come to realize how much advantage they might gain from joining us through conversion. Speak with any of the slaves or natives. You will find them outwardly docile, but look deep into their eyes, and you will see the stubborn stone of the devil still within them."

"If this is true, Francisco, then how do you deal with such intransigence?"

"Beatings sometimes. Starvation or other deprivations. It is always necessary to test the depth of their conversion, to be assured that they are not simply pretending to be Christians."

After dinner, I retired to my chamber to say my evening prayers. As always, my first prayer to God was thanks for my hidden secret. Only my mother and father knew of what they called my "shortcoming"; not even my brothers and sisters were ever told. I was named Diego De Herrera, the last child of my parents. They had not intended to have me, so my mother's pregnancy, later in her life, was a surprise. Then, my birth, two months earlier than expected, was another surprise. I came in the night, in the bed in which my parents slept, quickly and loudly, with no time to call the midwife. My father delivered me, and it was he who noticed I had only a single testicle. He told my mother that it was a sign that I would never carry forth the family name, and they decided in that moment to dedicate me to the Church.

They explained to me that I was special, meant for celibacy and religious service, but that I was never to reveal my special gift to anyone, for it would betray God's blessing on me because it meant taking pride in myself, a grave sin. I was obedient and devoted to them and, by extension, to the Church. I accepted without question the plan my parents insisted God had laid out for me. Only once, the night before I was to enter the monastery – I was sixteen – did I feel a physical sensation that I had never experienced. It was, I think, the excitement of my coming ordination into the Augustinian Brotherhood. I touched myself briefly and almost fainted from the thrill. When I fell asleep, I had terrible nightmares filled with moaning spirits and sobbing women. In that dream, I was slick with blood, being tossed among numerous hands that caressed and clutched at my body. The faces were blurred and strange to me because they were unnaturally white with red or blond hair and blue eyes. When I awoke, soaked in perspiration, I could still hear voices ringing in my ears saying, "*Cómeme para poder vivir de nuevo* – Eat me so I might live again." I told no one.

I awoke with a start. I had not thought of any of this for many years, so I was sure the long journey had simply exhausted me enough that I had let my guard down, allowing these memories to flood back. I thought that some cold water on my face would help and was drawn outside by the sound of soft guitars. I walked toward the music to find myself in a small square.

The fountain there bubbled quietly. The plaza was a replica of the squares common in Spain, although perhaps more simple and less elaborate. Its purpose was the same, however – to draw people together in a communal and social setting. I sat at the edge of the fountain and dipped my hand into the cool water.

There were almost twenty people there in the torch-lit plaza. Most seemed to know one another, standing in small groups of three or four, smiling and talking softly while two guitarists played in counterpoint to one another. I looked at their faces: only a few had recognizable Spanish features – creamy skin, aquiline nose, and slim torso. Most were darker, with broad, flat noses and more muscled bodies. The women tended to be heavier and dressed less formally than those I remembered in Spain. As conversations drifted around me, I caught some Spanish, but it was mixed with the unfamiliar words and pronunciations of the local patois.

"Are you new here, Fray?" a man's voice asked.

I turned to face the speaker, a young man dressed in a loose linen shirt and baggy pants. His hair was jet-black, and his skin deeply sun-tanned. "Yes. I arrived just today from Spain."

"But you are not one of the Franciscans," he said, looking at my robe. "They wear brown."

"Augustinian. We wear black," I explained.

"Is your group taking over for the Franciscans?"

"Why do you ask?" I answered, suddenly wary. I was being pumped for information when, in fact, I should be the one asking questions. I thought the young man too forward and without respect for my position as clergy.

He must have sensed my unease or heard the sharpness in my voice. He laughed, and his broad smile revealed gleaming white teeth. "I meant no offense, Father. I assume you have already met the Franciscans. If you've met Brother Francisco, I am his son." Again, the broad smile.

I did not betray my shock. *His son?* "He made no mention of family," I said coldly.

"Ah, my mother and I were part of his life as a conquistador."

I remembered Francisco telling me he had come to Veracruz as a soldier. He said that he discovered a preference for saving souls, which led him to a religious life. "You do not look like him," I said to the young man.

"I am *mestizo*," he explained. "Most of us inherit the look of our Indio or slave mother. Our Spanish fathers are seldom recognizable in our features."

"So, you and your mother must regret your father's surrender of his military life."

"Oh, no!" the young man responded. Again, he laughed. "My father understood that the best way to remain here with us was to become a religious. As a soldier, he would probably be sent elsewhere in the country to fight the natives. Here, as a religious, he has a good life and provides us with advantages as well."

"He has not renounced you as part of his past life?" I was uneasy with the relationship being described.

"Renounced?" The young man slapped his thigh in amusement. "Of course not! He divides his time equally between us and the Church. This is his solution to not abandoning us after he brought my mother to God."

I nodded numbly. Of course, there were religious back home who broke their vows of celibacy. It was not uncommon, and it was generally forgiven as long as it was relatively discreet. But Francisco apparently led two lives openly here in Veracruz.

"I am Tomàs," the young man said. "My father has always insisted that I be welcoming and respectful to all clergy."

I had to admit that his smile was engaging. "I am Friar Diego. Thank you for your welcome, Tomàs."

"I have another motive, however. I know that Father will be spending the night at the monastery because of your arrival. Could you please tell him that Mother wants him home later this week? He needs to prepare Rosalita, my little sister, for her Confirmation next month."

"Yes, I will," I mumbled. *There was another child?* I stood up as if to dismiss Tomàs. "I must return now." I retraced my steps back to my chamber, the soft guitar music seeming to mock my innocence and shock.

We were in Veracruz for more than a year, waiting not only for supplies from Spain but for the appearance of one of the 'Manila galleons' for the long journey to the Philippines. It was a good time for me to accustom myself to my life as a missionary, learning through experience about the ways of the natives and slaves. Always a quick learner, I picked up the native language quickly, and that marked me as one of only five friars who were chosen for missionary service in the Philippines. I listened to the local stories about the natives' lives before we brought them salvation, I learned about their societies and customs, and I was excited to begin my conversions.

On the other hand, something about this new land and weather troubled me in ways that I kept secret from my brethren because I believed they would think me insane. I again started to have anxious dreams about things that were foreign to me. For example, because Fray Francisco's family had free run of the monastery, their presence – especially his wife's – made my stomach churn with anxiety, although I did not know why.

Then, the dreams of long ago came back. At first, they were nothing more than flashes of visions coming to me when I was deep in prayer. Then, they expanded into nightmares without voices, people whose faces I had never seen, actions I had never experienced.

There were fields of heather and small herds of sheep. A pale young boy lay in the grass, daydreaming about the clouds above him. Then, dark clouds. The boy's face twisted with emotion, his breathing labored, until he suddenly moaned and lay still. He had a patch over one eye.

In other nightmares, heavy brocaded vestments pressed against my face until I could not breathe. Hands reaching for me as I ran between bookcases stuffed with scrolls and manuscripts. And finally, laying on my back feeling my warm blood spilling to the ground as birds circled overhead and children cried close by. And that terrifying plea: *"Quiero vivir de nuevo – I want to live again!"* This last image was always just before dawn when I would wake in a cold sweat, my right leg inexplicably cramped and stiff with pain.

I recognized none of the places in these visions, dreams, nightmares – whatever they were. Nor were any of the faces known to me, sometimes so twisted they hardly seemed human. I thought these were dangerous warnings of something, although I knew not of what. I revealed them to no one, sure that once I left Veracruz, I would leave these mental tricks of the tropics behind forever.

I will not recount the hardships of the journey across the Pacific in 1564 from Veracruz (via Acapulco) to Cebu in the Philippines, except to say that the five months' trip was almost unbearable. The hardships were the same as those from Spain to Veracruz except doubled by the length of the journey. Add to that the constant conflicts among the soldiers aboard; although some were true Spaniards, the majority were native recruits from New Spain.

I should not call most of them recruits. They were impressed into service by officers who wanted to be rid of them in Veracruz. They were *mestizos*, half-breeds whose Spanish fathers were gone from their lives if they ever were present at all. Some *mestizos* claimed their fathers had died or sailed back to Spain. Others admitted their fathers could not from the start be certainly identified from among the Spanish troops stationed in Veracruz, and still others – the smallest number – bitterly refused to name the fathers who had knowingly and callously abandoned them.

In short, they were a surly and unruly group, easy to take offense, petty and jealous over even the smallest material thing, and savage in demeanor. They were only allowed into the ranks of the conquistadors if they satisfied two requirements: they had to declare their conversion to Christianity, and their baptism had to be recorded with their Spanish father's surname (some, I suspect, chose such a name at random). Still, the pure Spanish conquistadors treated them as inferiors and, whenever possible, took advantage of them. Inevitably, then, there were always violent disagreements during the crowded and uncomfortable journey. The only advantage to me was that they continued to help me learn their patois.

I was, however, troubled as well by the pure Spanish conquistadors themselves. Many were, on close inspection, criminals escaping prosecution in Spain by enlisting. Some were young boys of similar age as I, who regarded their enlistment as nothing more than a chance for adventure and profit or perhaps a satisfaction of their desire to prove their manhood. Few, finally, had noble intent or a true Christian morality.

Happily, our navigator to the Philippines was Fray Andrés de Urdeneta, an excellent navigator. Although relatively old, he was ordered by King Philip to undertake the journey in order that Spain might establish its presence in the Philippines both commercially and religiously. Previously, Miguel López de Legazpi had established a colony on one of the islands, Cebu, after defeating the King, Rajah Tupas; it was the first European colony in the Philippines.

In Cebu, we learned of the larger island of Luzon far to the northwest and set our eye on the more favorable spoils of the Rajah: on the island of Luzon, we entered *Bahia de Manila* – Manila Bay – at dawn one day. It was a beautiful natural harbor, busy with ships of all sizes and shapes. Most I recognized as vessels of European origin, but there were also smaller, lighter boats that revealed a flourishing trading system prior to our arrival as Spanish conquerors. There were *dhows* from Arabia, *junks* from Japan and China with their bamboo sails like fans, and the Filipino *balangay*, the double-outrigger sailing ship used for trading.

Manila – *Maynila* to the natives - was Spain's – and, by extension, the Catholic Church's – primary presence in Asia. Legazpi built a fort called *Intramuros* here, and the Spanish colony grew quickly around it. The Augustinian friars were the first religious to arrive, and our austere black robes set us apart from the more colorful costumes of both Europe and Asia. We thought that the best use of our manpower was to become itinerant preachers throughout the surrounding areas of Manila, having been informed that Luzon, the island on which Manila sat, was the largest of this archipelago.

"You have already been noted for your linguistic abilities, Diego," Father Urdeneta said to me. "So, you must immediately set on the task of learning the language here."

"There are a variety of dialects, but I believe the primary one is called *Tagalog*. I will begin my studies immediately."

"Thank you. I must return to New Spain and, from there, to Spain itself," Urdeneta explained, "to make reports both to our Provincial Priory and to King Philip. I leave the care of these islands to my brothers in St. Augustine, but especially to Fray Martin de Rada, whose talent is in practical matters, and to you, whose talent in language and spiritual matters is unmatched. How shall you begin?" Urdeneta looked at me weakly; his eyes were failing, and his body was frail, seeming to waste away.

"There are some Spanish merchant families here in Manila; I shall entreat one of them to take me in and allow me to learn from their servants and slaves what I can. Once I feel confident with the language, I will start training other brothers so they might begin to spread Christ's word beyond the city."

"I would recommend the Galvez family to you. Señor Avelino Galvez is a rice merchant well-acquainted with these lands, and he moved his family here from Seville almost two years ago. He has prospered from his business acuity and is a devout Catholic; I am sure he will welcome you to his household." Urdeneta's conversation was interrupted by a coughing fit. He waved his hand at me in a gesture of dismissal. "Go with God."

I learned that Galvez owned numerous *palayan* – rice paddies – on the outskirts of Manila and spent much of his time overseeing their management. His family home, however, was in Manila, near *Intramuros*, so I sent a note there requesting an audience.

While I awaited word from Galvez, I familiarized myself with our Augustinian settlement here. A bamboo and nipa (palm leaf) church was built, San Augustin Iglesia. My compatriot, Martin Rada, had received word that he would be appointed the first prior provincial of the Augustinian settlement, called The Most Holy Name of Jesus. I was happy for Martin who distinguished himself as a defender of the natives; he continually sought ways to peacefully integrate their customs with our Spanish traditions. The natives I met in the markets of Manila were friendly and childlike, always smiling and welcoming.

Each evening before sleep, I'd write down the few words of Tagalog I'd learned, repeating them to myself as a way to commit them to memory.

I also prayed more fervently in Manila, both at Church and in my room in the monastery each dawn and at night, for my nightmares had not abated and, in some ways, were even worse. There was no coherent narrative to my dreams as if a story had been ripped from a book and the pages jumbled, out of order or lost. My visions were fragments; worse, their environments were unfamiliar to me, the personages blurred and strange: ordinary people and religious bickering, huge ships being torn down to their frames, rich clergy in brocade robes calling young boys and girls to them. And sometimes, a scroll unrolled by unseen hands, the carefully inked words squirming as if they were devoured by worms. Only one thing repeated itself, a phrase spoken in a whispered masculine voice: "*Cómeme para que pueda vivir* – Eat me that I might live." I did not understand its meaning; I only knew that it consistently frightened me awake, so that in the dark of my room, my eyes unsuccessfully sought the speaker in the shadows.

It was almost a month before Galvez answered my note, explaining that he had been abroad on business and had only recently returned home to Manila. He said he would be glad to meet with me at my earliest convenience.

The Galvez house was relatively easy to find because of its unique combination of European and Asian architecture. It was a wood and bamboo house (in Tagalog *bahay kubo*) built for the climate of the Philippines, resistant to both the rainy season and the earthquakes common to the area. The house was two stories: the living quarters occupied only the upper story which was supported on a rectangle of wooden posts. These posts were hidden behind thick wooden walls which hid storage rooms, offices, or cellars. The residence on the second floor had a narrow balcony, sliding windows made from capiz shells of oysters, and *ventanillas*, air vents below the windows. The roof was tightly thatched with nipa. Beside the narrow staircase leading up to the second-story residence was a wood statue of Santo Niño on a wall shelf, a copy of the statue given to Rajah Humabon of Cebu by Magellan when the Rajah was baptized as *Carlos*. I touched its outstretched hand briefly as I climbed the dark stairs.

There was no door at the top of the stairs, simply a doorway opening onto an expansive room containing a long wooden table and chairs with three woven nipa fans overhead. The windows were open to the late morning light.

"Hello?" I addressed the empty room.

"In the back," a male voice called from a room behind this main entrance.

I walked straight through into a smaller room, immediately noticing a short corridor beyond this space and rooms lighted by sunshine at the back of the house. "Hello," I repeated, stopping in the doorway. "I am Fray Diego de Herrera, here to see Señor Avelino Galvez."

A man seated at a desk stood up and smiled. "Please, call me Lino." He closed his hands in prayer and bowed his head, which I knew meant he wanted my blessing.

I put my hand on his shoulder and made the sign of the cross on him, saying, *"In nómine Patris, et Fílli, et Spiritus Sancti.* I am grateful you have agreed to meet with me, Lino."

Galvez showed me a seat and said he would find someone to serve us *lambanog*, a Filipino palm wine. He was a distinguished gentleman, clearly educated and wealthy. His clothes were European and, I noted, custom-tailored. I was surprised, however, to notice when he left the room that he was not wearing shoes.

"I believe you know this as *vino de coco*," he said when he returned, placing a cup before me on the table. It is the only wine we have in these islands but quite sufficient."

"Thank you," I said, taking a sip from my glass. "I am familiar with this since it is used in saying Mass here in Manila."

"Ah, yes, how could I not have known that?" Galvez shook his head. "A servant will bring some *merienda*," he added. "I have found it important to eat and drink frequently here in the tropics to remain hydrated."

I smiled, looking forward to an array of snacks before the heavier lunch meal. At the monastery, food takes a distant second place to spiritual nourishment. "I have come, Lino, to ask a great favor of you. Father Urdeneta recommended you and your family to me."

"He is a saint. Even more, did you know that he is a magnificent navigator?" Clearly, the priest's worldly skills were more impressive to Galvez than his spiritual skills.

"So I've heard, although I know nothing of sailing myself."

"If Spain is to flourish, we need to conquer as much of the world as possible."

"And bring the love of Christ to those who most need it," I added.

"Yes, yes," Galvez said, "of course, Fray." He cocked an eye at me. "Are you ordained as a priest?"

I bowed my head in humility. "Yes, but I prefer to serve as an itinerant friar-preacher. I serve Mass each day as required of my ordination, but I leave the administration of other sacraments to those who are better suited to those tasks."

"Ah, I see," Galvez muttered. "You are one of those who would rather convert and save souls than comfort those who are already within God's loving arms."

I had not thought of such a distinction myself, but I realized it was true. "Yes, you might say so, Lino."

"So, what is it you would ask of me?" He hunched forward.

He looked like he was negotiating with me. It made me uncomfortable as if we were bargaining in a business deal. I decided to start with a simple comment to make our discussion more congenial. "I see you wear no shoes."

"It is a local custom to remove one's shoes in the house. I find it charming."

"So you enjoy the native traditions?" Suddenly aware of my sandals, I tucked my feet under my robe.

"Not usually. This one happens to be quite comfortable."

"Well, I hope it is not too much to ask," I began hesitantly. "I'd ask shelter from you for a year or so, nothing more than a corner of your storage room downstairs, simple meals, and access to your servants and slaves."

"And in return?" He arched an eyebrow.

For a moment, I was mute with surprise. What could I possibly give him? "The blessing of the Church, certainly. And, since I say Mass every day, I would do it here at your house and welcome the presence of your family for your convenience."

"Not much of an equal relationship," Galvez said thoughtfully.

"Surely God's blessings have infinite value," I argued.

"Yes, of course, but I believe the teachings of the Bible: Give unto Caesar. . . ."

Here was, clearly, a man of the practical world. I was surprised but not upset. God bestows on us differing degrees of devotion. "I have been adequately tutored in classical studies since childhood. I could be a tutor to your children."

"Armando is already studying my business with me; he has had enough schooling. But Lydia," he stroked his chin, "she was lazy with schooling, wanting only to learn singing and dancing. Is there something you could teach her?"

"May I ask how old is she?"

"Fourteen," he answered. "She spends too much of her days twirling a fan and humming tunes."

"Perhaps some Bible study? Or literary study? I was

taught poetry appreciation."

Galvez shook his head. "Useless as far as I'm concerned. But it might fill her mind with something more valuable than daydreaming. All right." He sighed. "Teach her whatever you think might keep her interested for a time. How old are you?"

"Eighteen."

"Ah. Perhaps she will listen to someone closer to her own age."

"I promise an enriching curriculum," I said.

"But wait. Why do you want access to my servants and slaves? Of the latter, I only have two bought from a trader out of Jamaica. They are my blacksmiths for leather goods."

"Not your slaves, then, but your servants – they are natives?"

"Yes, all from this island, Luzon."

"I wish to learn Tagalog as well as the customs of the natives. Living among them is, I think, the most efficient way."

"They are all house servants here. Others work my *palayan* outside of Manila. The servants here live close by in nipa huts. Would that suit you?"

"Yes, it is exactly what I want. To be with them all day while they perform their services to you and your family. And to spend time with them in the evenings when they are with their own families. It would be quite perfect for my purpose."

"All right. We are agreed," Galvez said, standing and offering to shake my hand.

I nodded, and we shook hands. His grip was strong, but his palm was sweaty.

"Now, *merienda*," Galvez said, leading me back to the large room. The table was set with various fruit dishes along with a large platter of rice cooked with some carrot, egg, and onion. And there were small *empañadas*, fried golden and crisp.

"Come back tomorrow morning with your belongings. I'll make sure a place is made for you in a corner of the storeroom downstairs. I'll introduce you to the family at breakfast. Would eight be convenient?"

"Yes, fine," I answered as I bit into the warm *empañada*, the first I'd had for years, it seemed. "Thank you, Jesus Lord," I mouthed the words behind the napkin I used to wipe the tasty grease from my lips. It was only then that I noticed the two servants standing silently at either end of the long table, pulling gently and steadily on thin ropes that turned the huge fans above the table to cool Galvez and me comfortably as we ate.

The Galvez Household

On my arrival the next morning, just before eight, I was met by an older servant of the Galvez household, Juana Gabilado. I came to know her as the kindest and most honest of all the natives I had met in the Philippines. She was a devout Catholic and became the member of the household most protective of me, so I looked upon her, after a time, as my New World mother.

Señora Gabilado introduced herself to me with some reluctance. Haltingly, she said, "I am Juana Gabilado." She seemed wary and cautious of me.

"Señora, do you speak Spanish?" I asked, gently touching her arm.

"*Sí*, of course," she answered, stepping back from my touch. "Otherwise, how could I serve the Galvez family?" Now, she looked at me with impatience.

"I'm sorry, of course. I was not thinking." I shook my head at my own stupidity. "Perhaps you can speak Tagalog to me? I should like to learn your language." I smiled.

"The Master did not say that I should do so," she answered, "so it is not possible. Besides, I am very busy. Perhaps I can have one of my grandchildren accompany you through your day? They chatter ceaselessly."

"That would be wonderful. *Gracias, señora.*"

"The only *señora* here is Imelda Galvez. My name is Juana." There was a gentle reproof in her comment.

"Yes, Juana, I will not forget."

She showed me a simple bamboo mat in a corner of the cellar, next to which was a low table, a candle, and a chamber pot. I tucked my things into the corner: a change of clothes, my priestly things, and a notebook.

"You have no crucifix?" she asked. When I shook my head, she said, "I will make sure that one is hung on the wall for you."

Juana brought me to the Galvez *sala* to meet the waiting family. As soon as I entered the room, Imelda Galvez took my hands and squeezed them. "We are honored to have clergy in our house," she said. "These are my children, Armando and Lydia." She stepped back, allowing me to greet the children.

Armando was not a child – my age or a year older, I figured. He was seated casually, his legs stretched out before him. He did not rise to greet me but simply nodded in obvious boredom. Lydia, however, stood up and smiled. She was clearly a girl rather than a woman, although her gestures were already those of a young, single woman: she blinked her eyes frequently, and she fanned herself rapidly and coquettishly. "You are to be my tutor, I understand," she said breathlessly, her tone implying that, perhaps, I would be the one tutored.

I laughed and turned to the Señora Galvez: "I am sure that your daughter will find my tutoring quite instructive. She will learn much."

The *señora* nodded with satisfaction while Lydia sighed deeply and looked at me with clear disappointment.

During my first week in my new post, I discovered that the Galvez family was not very interested in me. They did not like to rise early for my Mass, preferring instead to only attend Sunday services in San Augustin Church at Intramuros. Some of the servants, required to be up early to prepare the household for the day, came to my Mass, glad that I would usually skip the sermon, which shortened the length of Mass considerably.

"*Ako si Efraim, tawagin mo akong Bong*" (I am Efraim, but call me Bong), the young boy said.

I had been washing my face at the barrel outside. I turned around to see a boy of not more than ten, barefoot and shirtless, standing behind me. "Where did you come from?" I asked, wiping my face on my sleeve. I only understood that his name was Efraim.

He knitted his brows and shrugged, clearly not conversant in Spanish. Then, slowly, he pointed to himself and said, "Efraim." He patted his chest and smiled, "Bong."

I grinned and pointed to myself. "Fray Diego."

"*Kain tayo,*" he said, pointing to the kitchen, then touching his fingers to his mouth.

Juana appeared in the doorway. "This is Efraim, but we call him Bong. He is inviting you to breakfast, Fray."

I nodded. *"Salamat, Bong."* I turned to Juana. "And thank you to you, too. Let's go."

I had coffee and a piece of toast in the kitchen with Juana while the house servants rushed around us to prepare and plate breakfast for the Galvez family. I spoke quietly with Juana, who often interrupted our cursory conversation with sharp words in Tagalog to the servants. Little Bong, who had seated himself beside me, ate two slices of toast with tomato and was reaching for a third when Juana slapped the table and said, *"Hindi, Bong!"* The little boy pulled his hand back into his lap.

"I think I have learned the word for 'No' in Tagalog, Juana," I said, smiling.

"This is the first time he has been allowed to eat such food, but he is being a glutton," Juana answered.

I reached for the toast with tomato and put it in Bong's hand. "Tell him this is my thanks for teaching me Tagalog," I said.

Juana shook her head, clearly disagreeing with me, but when she spoke to Bong, his face lit up, and he smiled widely at me. "You will never be rid of him now," she said to me.

Two hours later, I was instructed to sit with the Galvez family for breakfast. I was disappointed that the food was mostly Spanish: toast topped with fresh tomato, *embutidos*, and some reheated *empañadas* from the previous dinner. To one side was a platter of rice with bits of egg. "What is that?" I asked, pointing to the rice dish.

"A native staple. Rice with garlic and scrambled egg. It is not as oily as our usual dishes," Imelda Galvez offered. She put a spoonful on my plate. "If you like it, have more. Rice and eggs are most plentiful here in the islands."

Imelda fussed over the two children, adding or subtracting foods from their plates as she deemed necessary. Her ministrations of them went unchallenged.

Antonio ate his breakfast with singular concentration. It was clear that he had no wish to engage in conversation. As soon as his plate was empty, he stood up. "Pardon me, Mama. I must meet Papa at the docks." He bowed and left.

Lydia pushed her food from one side of her plate to the other, sighing heavily. "If I eat one toast, may I be excused? It is already too humid this morning."

I found the rice to be the most delicious of all that morning's offerings. It was seasoned lightly, and the eggs gave it a buttery flavor. "Lydia," I said, "have some of this rice. It's quite delicious, and it will help you to be alert for our first lesson today."

Lydia glared at me, then softened her gaze, realizing her mother was watching. "Thank you, Fray, but I am quite satisfied with the toast and a bit of coffee. And I thought we could postpone my lessons until after dinner when the weather is much cooler, making it easier to concentrate."

I looked at her mother, who did not seem to object to Lydia's proposal. And besides, I thought it would free my days for listening to and speaking with the house Filipinos. "What a splendid suggestion!" I looked at Imelda. "Lydia already impresses me as a good thinker."

Imelda nodded politely. She turned to Lydia. "You are excused." And, then, to me. "I have some household chores to oversee if you'll excuse me, Fray Diego." The two ladies left me alone at the table to plan my routine for the coming months.

Learning the native language was easier than I expected, in part because Tagalog had come into being as a means of communication for primitives. Once the natives came into contact with other cultures, they also added to their language, Tagalog, words for objects and activities that were previously unknown to them. This was true when the Chinese and the Arabs began trading in the Philippines but became much more pronounced with the Spanish. Perhaps, I thought, we Spanish were too lazy or too egotistical to throw ourselves completely into the native language; it was easier to force *our words* on Tagalog, just as we had, in our conversions and Baptisms, insisted that the natives take Spanish names, both personal and family. I was not sure that I approved or agreed, but I was certain that it was not a matter about which I wished to quarrel with my superiors.

At any rate, I realized that Tagalog – pre-Spanish Tagalog, that is – was a spare and limited language that was quickly enriched and expanded with the introduction of Spanish words. So, when the natives could not provide me with a Tagalog equivalent for one of my Spanish words, I simply recorded the latter as the official vocabulary, often with a small variation in spelling alone. To myself, I came to call this amalgam "Tagalish", which I spoke with greater frequency to the natives and which they, in their desire to please me, accepted and themselves adopted.

My linguistic studies being so easily completed, I turned my attention to the conversion of the natives and educating Lydia. In some respects, these were the same thing, for neither the natives nor Lydia seemed particularly devout to me. In fact, they were what I called "lazy Catholics" who did only what was required of them by Church rules. I suspected that, left to their own devices, they would lapse easily from their faith, foregoing Mass attendance or participating in Confession and taking the Eucharist, and finally, simply paying lip service to the Church without regard for the salvation of their souls. I recalled Friar Francisco's estimation of the native Indios in Mexico as "outwardly docile but. . . the stubborn stone of the devil still within them."

Lydia was like the rest except more. . . *exaggerated*, I guess I'd call it. The lack of devotion was more noticeable in her, perhaps because of her youth. She should have been more enthusiastic, more eager, it seemed to me. Instead, she had already, at the young age of fourteen, developed a kind of disinterested apathy about her Christianity, indeed about all of life itself. It disturbed and fascinated me at the same time, and I decided there was nothing more I wanted to do than to dispel in Lydia this lack of passion, this unwillingness to commitment of any sort. I thought to do so would mean that I needed to find something in her studies to interest her, to light a spark of some sort. But meanwhile, I also took it upon myself to bring the natives of the household to a greater fervor for Jesus Christ and His mother, our beloved Madonna.

To this end, I enlisted the aid of Juana, the only Filipina whose faith I did not question. She carried a wooden rosary, which she kept wrapped around her wrist and which, when she was idle, fingered as she silently prayed. "Idle" is certainly the wrong word here, for Juana seemed always to have something to do around the house. Only when she stopped for meals or had a brief *merienda* did she cease thinking about the Galvez house. So, while she sipped a coffee or broke off pieces of a sweet cake, she gently touched that rosary wrapped about her thin wrist and whispered wordlessly the prayer attached to each bead.

"What change do you think, Juana, would bring the household closer to God?" I asked her one bright morning as we sat on the veranda. Juana was preparing *lumpia* wrappers, a dough from which paper-thin crepes were made, to be filled later with small amounts of meats or vegetables and deep-fried.

At first, she shrugged, concentrating on combining the flour, cornstarch and water into just the right consistency. She kneaded the mixture with one hand while adding small amounts of water or flour with the other. Then, briefly looking up at me, she said, "You could teach us to read scripture, perhaps."

"But it is only in Spanish. It would mean that you first had to learn to read Spanish, Juana. And what of the others?

Those who speak only Tagalog?"

Again, the old woman focused her attention on the ball of dough in her bowl. Satisfied with its consistency, she stood up, intending to work the dough into thin sheets in the kitchen. "You are clever, Fray Diego. You will think of a way if you really want to bring us closer to God."

As the mosquitos buzzed around my ears, I realized that I had set an important task for myself – to begin translating into Tagalog those Church documents which would inspire the natives: some fervent prayers, stories of saints' lives, and perhaps some of the Latin Mass as well. It would be my life's work. Such a purpose, I hoped, would help dispel the nightmares that continued to plague me.

I decided it was easiest to begin with Lydia. She already spoke Spanish, so it would only be a question of finding the right materials to inspire her. Her youthful attitude was similar to the demeanor of the natives, who were, themselves, naïve in many ways. If Lydia's religious devotion could be awakened, so could theirs. My plan was to work on Lydia while I continued to become more fluent in Tagalog.

As Lydia had insisted, our lessons took place in the evening at eight p.m. before dinner. It was usually dusk when the lesson began and dark when it ended; the girl was right: it was cooler, making her concentration better and my patience with her greater.

Lydia could be a contrary girl, although not in a mean or cruel way. She was simply testing the limits of her independence as a girl on the cusp of adulthood. Or, at least, that is what I was told.

"You must be careful with the señorita Lydia," Juana advised me. I was sitting in the kitchen watching her pluck the feathers from a chicken she had just killed. The air smelled like the yard where the chickens roamed, and thin wisps of feathers floated around us.

"What do you mean, Juana?" I watched two small *butikis* chase one another up the wall and across the ceiling. These house lizards kept the mosquitoes to a minimum.

"She is a young girl, and you a young man." Juana concentrated on her task.

"I am a Fray, sworn to celibacy and uninterested in carnal pleasures."

"But that is not true of Lydia, is it, Fray?" Juana smiled at me.

"She is a young lady, Juana, well-bred. She would not dare." I shook my head to emphasize my answer.

"I only tell you to be alert. I accuse neither of you." Juana stood up and shook the chicken carcass to release the last of the feathers. She wiped her apron, and even more feathers floated through the rays of sunshine. Juana laid the chicken on the counter and picked up a sharp knife.

"I am more concerned with making her enthusiastic about her Christianity. I have tried reading Scripture with her, but she responds with apathy. I think I will see if stories of the saints' lives inspire her more."

"Here," Juana said, handing me an empty bottle, "please go to the cellar and fill this with vinegar from the vat. I'll need it for the chicken *adobo* lunch." She smiled again. "I only want you to be successful in your endeavors, Fray Diego," she said, indicating the subject was closed.

When I entered the cellar, I heard Bong singing softly. In the nine months he's been assigned to be my companion, I'd learned enough Tagalog to hold brief conversations with him. He was quick to correct me when we talked, but his corrections were always accompanied by his laughter as if I'd been meant to entertain him. He never made fun of my mistakes, simply found them amusing, and that put me at ease. "Bong?" I called out.

"Yes, Fray," he answered. "I'm here by your sleeping mat."

I went to fill the bottle with vinegar. "Are you going through my things again?" I asked. Bong was curious about me and would sit for hours simply looking through my meager possessions. He was especially fascinated by my notebook although he could not read.

"Yes, Fray, but I will not break anything," he said.

After I corked the bottle, I went and sat beside Bong in the dim cellar.

He wrinkled his nose. "You stink of vinegar," he said, laughing.

"Juana needs it for her *adobo*," I explained. "Come to the

kitchen. I'll find you something to eat." Bong seemed always to be hungry.

"No, Fray," he said, shaking his head. "Will you tell me what is on this page?" He pointed to the first page of my notebook which lay open in his lap.

"Shall I read it to you or teach you to read it?" The page contained only a few lines because I had designated it as the title page for my notebook.

Bong's eyes lit up. "You can show me how to read it?" He laid his small hand on the page like a caress.

"I will point to each word as I say it, and you can repeat it after me. All right?"

Bong nodded and seemed to hold his breath.

I read each word slowly: *Un cuaderno de mi estudio in tagalog por Fray Diego Herrera a los diez días de marzo 1564.* (A notebook of my study in Tagalog by Friar Diego Herrera on this tenth day of March 1564.) I smiled at Bong's wide eyes as if I were reciting a magical spell. "Now, repeat each word after me."

We read it together, and Bong put his finger under each word as he said it. "But what does it say?" he asked.

"What is the Tagalog word for this object?" I asked, pointing to the notebook.

"*Kwaderno.*"

We went over each word and created a transliteration of the words on the page. The only word I could not get Bong to give me the Tagalog equivalent of was "study." It was too abstract. Other than that, Bong seemed delighted to repeat the Spanish words over and over, underlining each word with his finger as he pronounced it.

"You did well, Bong. Now, do me a favor and bring this vinegar to Juana before she comes to scold me for not returning to the kitchen sooner."

He laughed again, took the bottle, and ran out. I closed my notebook and placed it under my pillow. I have already been in the New World for two years! I shook my head. I had not accomplished as much as I'd hoped. The realization made me more determined to step up my plans to bring all those within my range of influence much, much closer to God, to make them all so devout that their entrance into heaven would be guaranteed.

"May I see her picture?" Lydia asked quietly, leaning towards me.

"It is a drawing of St. Catherine of Siena," I explained, pushing the pamphlet across the table to Lydia. "She is depicted here giving her heart to Christ. It was painted by an Italian named Giovanni di Paolo." I had found the slim booklet in the library in Manila; the abbot explained it had come from the Augustinian library in Seville, along with other hagiographic materials. I was delighted that we had stored some detailed biographies of various saints that included drawings of the subjects, and that the abbot allowed me to borrow them.

"She is so beautiful," Lydia said, running her finger along the outlines of the woman's face.

"Her beauty reflects the depth of her devotion to God," I explained.

Lydia sighed. "Was she a nun?"

"No, a lay woman who devoted her life to God nonetheless. Her parents wanted her to be suitably married, but she resisted."

"How?" Lydia leaned forward with interest.

"First, she cut her hair to make herself less attractive. And she made herself frail with fasting."

"Oh," Lydia whispered with disappointment. Clearly, she liked eating and being pretty.

"Then, when her mother tried to improve her health with a visit to the healing baths, she fell seriously ill with a rash and fever. That convinced her parents to allow her to join a group of devout women, called the *Mantelle*."

"And so she never married. A woman," Lydia said with admiration, "of independence."

"What are you thinking, Lydia?"

"I think I would like to become like St. Catherine, to devote myself to God in some way."

"You mean to live a life of solitude and almost total silence with your family? That is what Catherine did, dear girl. She gave herself over wholly to Jesus Christ, even wearing on her finger a piece of his body as a holy relic." I thought it too indelicate to explain to Lydia that the holy relic was Christ's foreskin, which Catherine wore as a wedding ring. I stifled a laugh. Lydia had neither the intelligence nor the spirituality of St. Catherine. She was an ordinary girl, the daughter of ordinary parents. I expected nothing extraordinary from her, only a fervent devotion to God. "I think your parents have other plans for you, dear girl."

"We are in a new world, Diego. What my parents want may be irrelevant."

I was unpleasantly surprised that she had addressed me so familiarly; even more, she was expressing a rebelliousness I had not anticipated in her. "Hush, now. That is no way for a young lady to speak."

"And you are too young to scold me for my words," Lydia replied. Despite her comment, she lowered her eyes, wary of directly confronting me.

"I am your brother's age, yet I have already traveled over the world and gained experiences that neither you nor your brother could imagine." I squared my shoulders. "Look at me, Lydia. You must see that I am your teacher, and your defiance displeases me greatly." I blushed, never having taken such a tone with anyone before.

Lydia looked up. "And you must see," she said, covering my hand with one of hers, "that I only want you to see me as a young woman who wants to please other than simply my parents." She squeezed my hand. "I am ready to love."

"I want what's best for you, Lydia," I said less sternly, placing my free hand atop hers. "You must understand that."

Lydia looked down at our hands, folded one on top of the other, and smiled. "This is the first time you show that you like me."

I quickly withdrew my hands, folding my arms across my chest. "You mistake my concern." But I blushed again, and with the realization that Lydia assumed I was being affectionate, my body stiffened. "Our lesson is over. Good night, Lydia." I withdrew the hagiography material from her. "You are dismissed."

Lydia sat in silence for a moment, then rose and shrugged. "I go to bed, Fray." She laughed softly. "But I think I will dream of Diego."

I quickly retreated to my mat in the cellar. I lit no candle, unwilling to acknowledge the heat I felt in my body. I undressed and knelt on my mat, peering disconsolately into the dark. I took my thick-woven belt and wrapped one end tightly around my fist. I gritted my teeth and started the self-flagellation that I had been taught as a novice.

"You are a man and will have urges, sexual feelings," the novice-master had explained.

"Not I, sir. I was born deformed, lacking part of my genitals. My father said I was incapable of sexual appetites." I had lifted my robe to show the master that I was missing a testicle.

"Nonsense," he had said, reaching for me and rubbing me vigorously. "You see," he announced triumphantly, pointing to my erection, "you are capable of the same sin as any man. And we have the perfect atonement."

Then, he had turned me around, pulled my robe off, and pushed me to a kneeling position. With his knotted belt, he had lashed my back, each time saying, "God forgives you."

At first, the beating confused me. The novice-master had

aroused me then whipped me. The arousal was disturbing, but it felt good; the whipping hurt, but it, too, ultimately felt good, for it relieved the arousal through ejaculation. That sexual appetite had been awakened, satisfied, and dissipated.

Not since my novitiate had I felt such urges, and I realized it was because I had not been in circumstances that tempted me, until now. So, in the muggy dark of the tropics, far from home, I beat myself as I had been taught. It was to tame the beast in me, as well as to ultimately expel it. Did I, like the ignorant natives, like the still-innocent Lydia, have the devil inside of me? Was I no better than they were? No! I was beyond them, for I had an answer to the evil within: surrendering to pain resulted in redemption.

When I laid down to sleep, my back stinging with welts, I started to realize that pain was the only certain way to redemption. We expiate our sins and guilt through suffering; our willful suffering is the manifestation of our true devotion. I knew now how I was going to bring these people to God's bosom.

That night, my dream-nightmares recurred, but now I found a kind of fevered peace in them. I understood that the suffering and pain, the violence and bloodshed, all the horrors of the dream were steps in the path to a divine and liberating salvation. It was as if my God was inviting me to a eucharist more mystical than any I had ever partaken.

And when I awoke just before dawn, bathed in the sweat of those dreams, I felt anew the stinging of the salty perspiration in my wounds, and I smiled. The pain was exhilarating, a kind of satisfaction that soothed me. *"Gracias, mi Dios."*

Conversion

I continued to tutor Lydia. Although I taught her daily, giving her catechism materials to read or memorize, and instructing her about the women in the Bible who suffered greatly because of their disobedience, I kept her at a distance, physically and emotionally, by telling her about the women I had met in Spain who were far more beautiful and grander than she could ever be. I led her to believe that she was completely unattractive to me, dull and boring. It did not take her long to lose interest in me, and our lessons became nothing more than ordinary routine.

I admitted to no one that Lydia's initial attraction to me and her clumsy attempt at seduction had awakened in me those base sensual appetites that I had thought were contained and controlled long ago. However, nightly prayers with lashes helped. In addition, I fashioned out of some wire mesh a cilice which I wore on my thigh under my robe. Whenever I felt a corporeal desire – whether for food, drink, or touch – I pressed on the cilice to remind myself that denial was the path to righteousness.

And I set my sights on the more easily persuadable target of little Bong. He was young enough that I needn't worry about first dispelling his bad habits; he was the *tabula rasa* on which I could imprint a true and unswerving devotion to our Lord. Of course, because he was just a little boy, I had to enact my plan gradually; I wanted his conversion to be irreversible.

I began to spend almost every waking hour with the boy. He was a quick learner, a quality his family seemed not to care much about, because they were more impressed with strength than intellect. They survived by farming, a grueling routine of planting and harvesting rice, retrieving fruits from the tall coconut and jackfruit trees, and reclaiming small bits of land from the ever-encroaching jungle. Bong was one of fifteen grandchildren of Juana Gabilado; she chose him as my companion because he would not be particularly missed in his large family.

"I will call you Efraim, your Christian name," I told him.

"Do you know why you are so named?"

"No, Fray. I think the priest at church named me at my baptism."

"So, your birthday is January 28, eh?"

The boy's eyes widened with surprise. "How did you know? Are you a *mangkukulam*?"

I laughed. "I am no sorcerer, Efraim. You were named on the day the Church celebrates St. Ephraim of Syria, a writer of hymns and verses." I tousled his hair. "Perhaps you will also compose songs, hmm?" The boy was always humming a tune around the household.

"I like to sing. My favorite part of the Mass is the chanting, Fray." His dark brown eyes shone with the memory.

"Well, I have an idea. You will teach me Tagalog at the same time that you learn Spanish, and we will do this by learning a catechism. And perhaps I will teach you a Latin chant, too. All right?"

"What is a catechism, Fray?"

"A way of learning. It consists of questions and answers. It will be fun, Efraim, you'll see!"

"I don't understand, Fray, pardon me." He frowned, his small face wrinkling on itself.

I smoothed out his expression by pulling his mouth into a smile. "Here is my question," I started and gently squeezed the boy's shoulder. "Who made you?" I asked in Tagalog.

Efraim shrugged and scratched his head. "Is this like a riddle?"

"No, dear boy. The answer is 'God made you.' You must repeat that back to me in Spanish. Say, *Dios te creó.*"

He hesitated, licked his lips, then slowly repeated in Spanish what I had said.

I tousled his hair again. "Excellent, Efraim!"

And so we went on slowly, starting with the most basic of Catholic precepts, such as why did God make us? And what must we do to save our souls? With each question and answer, both Efraim and I became more fluent in each other's language, and that sharing brought us closer as companions. For an hour or so each morning, I would compose the series of questions and answers for the day, then when Efraim and I sat at breakfast (which Juana prepared for us), we would have our catechism class while Juana, although attending to her kitchen chores, listened and often smiled with pride at the boy's (and my) progress.

Each day, I would send Efraim home at lunchtime with the excuse that his family needed him for a few hours. I would see him again at three or four in the afternoon when we would walk through the fields or in the village, and Efraim would explain to me whatever I inquired about – whether the names of neighbors and animals, or how to open a coconut – and I would scribble notes in my small journal.

When Efraim was gone home at midday, I excused myself from the noon meal and retired to my mat in the basement. When I was sure everyone was either out or having their siesta, I used my lash and tightened my cilice while whispering prayers of atonement, for I had grown too fond of the boy, too proud of his quick wit, and too affectionate for his well-being. I knew this to be sinful, for everything I felt about Efraim I should have been giving to God, my Lord and Savior. Thus did I, each day, renew my own devotion as well as groom Efraim to greater religious dedication.

Once the boy became accustomed to our routine, I began to fashion more difficult questions to answer, whether the difficulty was in the concept or simply in the language itself. In short, I started to challenge the boy: could he understand abstract ideas about love or penitence, or would his primitive language provide actual words for the nuances of sophisticated Spanish? When there was a gap, or a loss, of understanding, I introduced discomfort to Efraim. Did he not understand the difference between venal and mortal sin? I would smack the back of his head as a sign of my displeasure. Could Tagalog not verbalize omniscience? I would tug on the boy's ear, pinching it until it reddened.

When Efraim would recoil from these small chastisements, I would rub his head or stroke his ear and kiss him lightly. "I can make you feel better when I stop, eh?" It was in this way that I gave the boy the opportunity to understand the connection between pain and pleasure, that the pleasure was always greater if it followed on pain. It was the same lesson I had learned myself: to feel good, I needed first to feel the pain of the whip or cilice and to realize that the pain was a necessary prerequisite for experiencing relief and even liberation from sin.

It was more than two years that I spent with Efraim learning Tagalog and the customs of the Filipinos. He was approaching the age of twelve which, he explained to me, was important in their culture as the age at which he officially left boyhood and became a man. "I must change my ways, Fray."

I was amused that this boy, at age twelve, was expecting to suddenly become a man just because of a birthday. "And how will you do that, Efraim?"

"I will burn the cut foreskin and then bury it in the jungle. That symbolizes the end of my childhood."

"What?" I asked, taken by surprise. "You will burn *what*?"

"My foreskin," Efraim said, pushing down his shorts. "This," he said, pulling at the sheath of skin that covered his penis. "The *matatanda* – elders – will cut some of it off."

"What?!?" I demanded. "You cannot do this, Efraim. It is called circumcision, and it is strictly forbidden by the Church."

"But it must be done or I will never be a man." Efraim pulled up his shorts. He looked worried.

"Efraim, the Church accepts those who are already circumcised, but it frowns on continuing the practice. Do you understand?"

"No, Fray. You cannot ask me to disobey my parents. In three or so months, when I reach twelve, it must be done."

Within weeks, I sat down with the Abbot at Intramuros. "Father," I started, "I have a boy soon to be circumcised."

"And you want to stop it," he answering, smiling.

"Of course! We are taught it is what distinguished us from the Jews who tortured and killed our Lord, Jesus."

"Yes, yes," the Abbot responded. "But be calm, Fray."

"I wish to save the boy," I said.

"It is not the way to bring these pagans to Christ," he answered. "We live in the sixteenth century, a time of great discovery and exploration. If we are to enamor ourselves to the whole world, we must make certain allowances and practice inculturation."

"It is a barbaric practice," I insisted.

"What harm does it bring to the Church or to the practitioner?"

"It is a sin," I repeated.

"The Church condemns many actions, Fray, but it does not automatically declare such condemnations as sins. This circumcision matter is a perfect example. Let it go; you will see that your tolerance will make people more receptive to your Christianity."

I left Intramuros disconsolate. Was I being abandoned by my own people? How could I reconcile what I had been taught with what I was now being told to accept? By the time I arrived back at the Galvez compound, I was filled with confusion.

That night, after Lydia's lesson, I sought out her father. "I am feeling a little sick, perhaps a touch of malaria. May I have a cup of *vino de coco*? I think it will help me to sleep and recover."

"Of course," Avelino said, telling a servant to fetch a cup

for me.

"And would it be possible to have the boy, Bong, stay by me tonight? If I become sick, he can fetch the doctor."

"I'll have Juana send him to you. It's a good precaution, Fray. Also, be sure to use your mosquito net tonight."

"Thank you, Señor Galvez. I wish you a peaceful rest tonight." I bowed to him and carried my wine to the cellar.

When Efraim appeared, bare-chested and wearing only shorts, he was rubbing his eyes. "My grandmama woke me, Fray, and told me to come straight here. Is something wrong?" The boy's hair was sticking up in spikes all over his head.

"You need to stay with me tonight, Efraim. I must talk with you about something very important."

"What is it, Fray?" he asked, sitting next to me on my mat. The single candle fluttered in the hot night breeze, throwing soft shadows across his face.

"First, drink some of this. It will relax you." I handed him the cup of wine.

He sipped at the wine. "This has been forbidden to me, Fray," he said, holding the cup out for me to take back.

"No, no. Tonight is special. You must drink it, dear boy." I gently pushed at his outstretched hand. "And let me teach you the chant I promised." I smiled. "But we must say it softly so as not to wake or disturb anyone."

The boy took a long swallow and smiled.

"It's in Latin. I will translate for you, but then you must learn the Latin by continually repeating it to me, all right?" I laid my hand on his shoulder. "And you must sit with your back against the wall and your legs stretched out." I tapped on his legs folded under him.

"I am ready," Efraim said, taking another long swallow. He rearranged his body as I directed. I noticed in the candlelight that his ears were tinged red. "But I am feeling very hot."

"It is the wine relaxing you, boy. Now, the chant is 'Lamb of God, who takes away the sins of the world, have mercy on us.' And in Latin: *Agnus Dei, qui tollis peccata mundi, miserere nobis.*" I leaned in towards him. "Whisper, Efraim, and relax."

I not only wanted to show the boy that his planned circumcision was unnecessary for him to become a man but also that what I would teach him was a method of spiritual redemption. I had decided to do this even if it meant I was committing a sin myself; I could redeem myself through self-flagellation.

While Efraim whispered the *Agnus Dei*, I soothed him until he finished the wine. He was a young boy and slight of stature; the liquor quickly put him in a stupor. I reached into his shorts and massaged him as the novice master had done for me so many years before. Efraim's resistance was immediate but feeble. I whispered the chant with him, further garnering his helpless acceptance. And when I heard his moaning, having had aroused him fully, I said, "Now you will feel some pain, but remember that it will turn to pleasure quickly. Do not shout out."

I rolled the boy onto his stomach and drew myself into a kneeling position. Earlier that evening, I had stripped some palms from the trees, fashioning a kind of thin whip. With that instrument, I lashed the boy's back until welts sprung up.

He moaned louder until I place my hand lightly over his mouth. "Keep chanting. Think of God's goodness. He will soon release you from the pain."

I hit him again until he shuddered. Then, I lifted his body and held it close to me, briefly touching his shorts to feel the damp spot there; I was assured of my success. "God is realized, Efraim. He welcomes you as a man into his company. Now you know how to sin and how to be forgiven your sin." I hugged him until he went limp. "Now, sleep."

I kept Efraim with me that night. In the morning, when I woke, I found him squatting beside me, his head lowered. "How are you feeling?" I stretched lazily.

"Something bad. I did something bad," he muttered.

"Nonsense, Efraim. Look at me and smile." I sat up and put my hand under his chin.

"You are now a man, Efraim, without the cutting. Tell your mother that God rejoices in you, that the unchristian ceremony must not be done. Later, I will teach you how to use the palm leaves by yourself to relieve you of any sin you might be tempted toward. I am so proud of you!" I squeezed his shoulder.

"I feel different," he said quietly.

"Of course you do. It is God's grace flowing through you." And I led him to the kitchen to fetch breakfast.

Spreading the Faith

Efraim's conversion was gradual. With my admonitions, he kept the manner of his conversion secret, but I had to spend weeks justifying to him the value of his experience. Any sin he committed, I explained, as long as it was unintentional, could be forgiven with the application of the palm leaves. "So, for example," I said, "you see a girl and feel a stirring in your loins. Perhaps you even kiss a girl or touch her in a moment of mindless passion. Just find a private place and give yourself enough lashes until the pain is replaced by relief."

Eventually, he came to see that this method of negating sin was efficient and convenient. He managed to resist his parents' insistence on his circumcision, and they finally surrendered to my cautions that Efraim was thus guaranteeing his place in heaven. They were relieved when they saw no adverse effects on the boy.

"Do you think, Fray, that I could teach this to some of my friends?"

For a moment, I wanted to forbid him to do so. But then, I thought it might be a good idea. "You must be cautious about this, Efraim. Many will not understand or agree."

"So, you don't want me to tell anyone?"

"You must be discreet. Choose only boys, never girls. And the boys must be younger than twelve, so uncircumcised. And you must be sure that they trust you, and you can trust them."

"The *vin de coco* helped a lot, Fray," he said, smiling.

"At least for a while, you should bring the boys to me first, Efraim. I can better judge if they are susceptible to conversion."

"Of course, Fray."

I had been in the Galvez household for three and a half years. I had become relatively fluent in Tagalog and converted all of the household workers and their families, either through traditional methods or through my special conversions (with

Efraim's help). It was time to move on, and so I asked Provincial General Martin de Rada if I might be assigned somewhere else in the islands.

He sent me to Cebu, almost three hundred miles south of Manila. It was an island ruled by a Moslem rajah, Tupas, who remained the civil leader of his people although he had bowed to Spanish rule three years earlier in 1565. It was easy for me to learn the local dialect, Bisayâ, which we called *Cebuano*, since I had mastered Tagalog earlier. For two long years, I preached zealously to these people, most of whom practiced a syncretic form of Hinduism and Animism.

Five years in Cebu were uneventful, more like a long and drowsy hibernation for me. I tended to the natives but found them dull and unresponsive in any meaningful way. Unlike the Tagalogs on Luzon, these *Cebuanos* were recalcitrant, unwilling to surrender their pagan ideas, unenthusiastic about what my rich Spanish culture could teach them.

So, we played a game of mutual deception: I pretended to accept them as true converts, and they pretended to accept Jesus Christ as their true savior. I taught no one what I had taught to Efraim; I deemed none of them worthy, for this was an inferior flock that inspired nothing more than tedium in me. I lied in my missives to Manila, sending embroidered letters of glorious conversions and miraculous transformations; and these prevarications I pardoned in my usual and secret way, with whips and chains on my body.

If any part of my life retained any spark of excitement, it was when I slept. The nightmares became more vivid, more detailed. The characters developed personalities, mostly cruel and threatening: an old man whose bitterness made him distrustful, a high Church official who satisfied his lusts on those under him, and a cripple who reveled in unspeakable perversions. More and more, it was this last personage who dominated my nightmares until I would be startled awake with a final image of his incredible joy at being torn limb from limb, all the while whispering, "Take me to be reborn."

Much to my relief, my otherwise five dreary years in Cebu were suspended by the Prelate's order for me to return to Spain to recruit candidates for missionary work in the Philippines. I would choose a contingent of fifty or so brothers, begin teaching them Tagalog and Bisayâ, and prepare them for their work in the Islands. I had thought my request for transfer to Cebu was a mistake, but now I realized it was necessary for my promotion to being a leader of men. I balanced my pride with my secret self-punishments.

I landed back in Mexico in 1575, almost two years later, eager to board our galleon, *Espiritu Santo*, to Manila. Anxious to return to the Philippines, I was also disappointed that of the forty brothers assigned to me in Spain, only six could continue on to Manila. The rest were either too frail after the Atlantic crossing or too easily felled by the tropical weather, and they were required to remain in Mexico.

I was further disheartened to hear that my old friend, Fray Francisco, had died of typhus the year before. I sought out his son, Tomas, finding him in a small shack at the edge of town, the father of three children and husband of a sickly wife. I brought a bottle of tequila with me, but on arrival, was sorry I had not thought to also bring bread and *chorizo*.

"Tomas, I give you my condolences about your father. What of your mother?"

"She was no longer welcome among the Franciscans. She returned to her Indio tribe in the jungle with my younger siblings." Tomas shrugged. "Thank you for the tequila. You seem to be healthy." He placed the bottle on the table. "Shall we drink together?"

"No, I have never much liked tequila, so keep it for yourself." I patted his arm. "You are married now and a *papa*?"

"A father, yes. Married, no. What need to pay the Church for a ceremony? It did my mother no good in the end."

I shook my head. "You are bitter, Tomas. You were not this way when we first met."

"I have learned the ways of the conquered, Diego. What we are given is only at the whim of the conqueror, and when we are no longer useful, what has been given is taken away." He nodded towards the mother of his children, sitting silently in a corner. "I stay because the Christians taught me to stay with the mother of my children, and I was stupid enough to be persuaded."

I was sorry for him, but I also knew that his misery had been visited upon him by God, who does no wrong. Tomas was suffering because his father had ignored his vow of celibacy, had sought no penance for his wrongdoing, and had died without remorse. "When I return to the cloister, I'll make sure that some food is sent to your children from their stores." I could offer little more. "May I bless you?" I asked, standing, hoping that my bestowal of God's blessing would bring Tomas some relief.

"Don't bother, Fray. Your words would fall on unyielding stone." His remark convinced me he was truly his father's son but yet an Indio.

That night in my bed, I thought about all the changes that had occurred. Eleven years ago, I'd arrived in Mexico eager to proselytize for Christ. I discovered my talent for language, which benefitted my wish to preach as well as my career as a religious. And, most of all, I was sure that I could somehow share my love for Christ through acts of charity and generosity. Perhaps I expected too much of the *Indios* both here and in the Philippines. They did not readily see the values we offered them, both materially and spiritually, and often wanted to cling, instead, to their primitive ways. I turned to the wall, too tired to get up to say my night's prayers. Instead, I simply pressed on the cilice that I always kept wrapped on my thigh. As I applied pressure and felt the sharp pain, I moaned quietly and closed my eyes, resigned to the nightmares of flesh being torn apart by bony hands and the sound of lips smacking in hungry anticipation. I endured this knowing that, ultimately, I would feel pleasure and satisfaction.

Just before I fell asleep, I remembered that tomorrow would be my twenty-ninth birthday.

Mere days after my birthday, we were deposited onto the *Espiritu Santo* bound for Manila. It was mid-March, and with favorable northerly trade winds, we were expected in Manila before the end of July. Despite my upbringing, my education, and my strong faith, I could not shake a superstition that gripped me about this galleon.

On the day of boarding, I offered to bless the boat and its journey, but the captain refused. He said that it would be *mala suerte* – bad luck – to bless *un galeón maldito* – a cursed galleon. That is, he had petitioned the Royal Court to keep the galleon's true name, *San Juan*, but his request was refused. It seems that twenty-one years earlier, in 1554, a galleon named *Espiritu Santo* shipwrecked off the coast of Texas while carrying men and goods from Veracruz, Mexico to Havana, Cuba. All aboard, crew and passengers, as well as cargo, perished, sinking into the Gulf of Mexico without a trace. This boat, the *San Juan*, had been just recently rechristened as a memorial to that galleon.

The captain said that most of the original crew – mostly loyal Spaniards – disappeared once the *San Juan* was renamed; they believed that this ship was destined for tragedy. The captain had difficulty finding a trustworthy crew, and finally had to use many *Indios* of Malaysia and the Philippines as replacements, some of them slaves or desperate men. They sailed not for the glory of Spain or God, but for freedom or whatever treasure they believed they could personally gain. He warned me as we sailed out of the harbor, "Sleep with a weapon, Fray. And clutch your crucifix as well."

Besides the crew, there was a contingent of soldiers and their commandant to replenish the Manila garrison, some government administrators to replace those whose tenure had expired, and myself and my six Augustinian brothers, most of whom were young men as I had once been.

The ship was also packed with goods: silver bullion and coin, lace and other cloth from Mexico and Spain, as well as those various items ordinary in Europe but unavailable in the

Philippines. Additionally, the captain and his officers were commonly known to smuggle goods for their personal profit beyond their normal pay: gems and medicines being the most prized. I had to continually assure my young and inexperienced brothers that as long as they raised no objections to the actions or behavior of the crew, they would arrive in Manila safely.

Meanwhile, the ship sailed uneventfully along its northwesterly route across the Pacific, its population living warily of one another; arguments and physical fights were not uncommon but manageable by the intercession of either the officers or the soldiers. We friars said Mass every day, but only a few attended – either those who owned nothing worth stealing or those who hired personal guards from among the soldiers onboard. We were a community of travelers in only one sense: we were all uneasy with the voyage because of the rumors about the ship being cursed, and we simply wanted to reach landfall as soon as possible.

Little more than a month into our journey, we sighted the island of Guam. More than half of the crew expected us to stop there, hoping to jump ship, thus gaining their freedom. But the captain, still certain that the ship was destined for some catastrophe, refused to dock there, believing that the natives, the *Chamorros*, were untrustworthy.

He was not mistaken. Those natives were indigenous to the Marianas, an island group north of Guam. The Spanish had brought such widespread war and disease to those islands that they started to relocate the Chamorros, who had converted to Christianity to Guam. Many suspected, our captain included, that the conversion was one of convenience and survival rather than sincerity or devotion. Thus, we sailed past Guam while much of the crew grumbled. We still had three months of ocean ahead.

The captain began to relax once we entered the Philippine Sea, which marked the western edge of the Pacific. And so we settled into an uneasy boredom with the journey and our companion passengers. We had traveled more than thirteen hundred miles from Guam without incident. Perhaps our superstitions had, indeed, been unwarranted.

Except that we'd been wrong. Barely in sight of the island of Catanduanes, an outer atoll of the Philippines, we encountered a squall which drove our galleon, heavy with cargo and passengers, toward the jagged reefs. Suddenly, everyone who had thought the ship was cursed was now sure that disaster was imminent. Thus, the captain's orders, the officers' commands, and the crew's actions were nothing more than the acts of defeated men: they could not believe that anything they did would change their fate, and so their actions were half-hearted at best. Within two hours, the ship was breached by the sea's treachery, and all our efforts turned to saving our lives rather than rescuing the *Espiritu Santo*.

There was chaos, loud and cruel. My only order to my small group of brothers was, "Save yourselves as best you can. Swim toward land. Pray to God." The soldiers were the first to abandon ship, jumping into the sea fully armored and clutching their weapons. They were followed by the administrators, clutching papers wrapped in oilcloth, their pockets bulging with whatever precious things they could hold. Then, the brothers, trembling and mumbling prayers, their eyes wide with fright. When I jumped into the water, my heavy robe an almost unbearable weight in that choppy water, I found a piece of the ship to cling to and floated there, watching those around me scrambling for purchase on the flotsam that fell from the galleon, and observing the crew leaping free of the sucking eddies that the sinking boat created.

Landfall – the island – was in sight but only as a small bump on the horizon. Many of us who tried to swim quickly exhausted ourselves; the lucky ones found something to float upon, but the rest simply sank silently into the sea. Whenever I thought the current was carrying me away from that strip of land, I paddled myself toward it until my legs ached. It was July, and this was the tropics. We had shipwrecked in the late afternoon. I knew that nightfall would not come for hours, but then it would be suddenly dark, more would die in the water and no doubt the predators would come, particularly the reef sharks and the moray eels. "We must head for shore," I shouted, hoping that some would hear me. "God still needs you!" I said, thinking that this might spur some to fight for survival. And I started swimming, pushing ahead of me the simple fragment of wood, a vestige of our cursed ship.

Less than twenty of us, a mix of religious, crew, and a few soldiers, made it ashore alive. Others arrived as dead bodies washed up onto the golden sand. None of the administrators survived, nor any of the officers; most of the soldiers drowned in their armor. The surviving soldiers and crew, none of them Spanish, spoke to each other in a patois of Tagalog, Bisayâ, and Malay. I understood only a few of their words – "freedom," "death," and "escape" – but I went to each of them to bless them, congratulate them with a smile and a squeeze of their shoulders, and said to them, *"Manalnagin kasama ako sa Diyos"* – Pray thanks with me to God. Most nodded as if they understood.

I knew the island was inhabited and found it strange that the natives had not come to help us or greet us. Nevertheless, I urged the surviving three brothers to scour the beach for branches and vines or seaweed with which we could fashion a cross. "Meet me there," I said, pointing to a small jetty of rocks. "Will we give thanks to God with a cross and attract the attention of the natives."

While our small group sat shivering in the brief twilight, wishing for a fire, for dry clothes, for some food and water, I found one of the crew who spoke Spanish, so he could convey my words to the others who did not. "We will be rescued, I am sure, by the natives here. And later, Manila will send out a search party to bring us safely to Intramuros."

Someone asked how far we were from Manila. "About two hundred miles, I think," I answered. Most of the distance was overland, so it meant traversing a great deal of jungle. "It might be about a week," I added, "but I am sure we will find shelter with the natives tonight." I turned to the young brothers anchoring a makeshift cross into the rocks. "Let us pray now."

We gathered in a semicircle around the cross, knelt, and faced the ocean, now becoming dark with the night sky. I could hear the waves rolling gently onto the shore.

"First, we pray for those who did not survive, both those asleep deep in the sea and those who the waves carried silently to this shore." We bowed our heads for a moment. "And now we pray for ourselves, saved by God to serve his purpose here on earth." I made the sign of the cross over the group.

I heard someone behind me clearing his throat. When I turned, I saw a large group of natives standing in the sand. They carried spears and machetes, as well as two or three torches. "Our earthly saviors have arrived," I said to my group of survivors who turned as one to see.

"We are happy to see you," I said in *Cebuano*, expecting these natives to know Bisayâ, the dialect of the southern provinces. "Do you know that some of us are religious – Friars – who have experienced dangers, hardships, and storms to save your souls? We want only your assistance until Manila comes to retrieve us." I smiled broadly.

They whispered among themselves, but I could not hear what they were saying, not even sure that I would understand their dialect. One stepped forward toward me. He was not old, but certainly older and stronger than the others. His chest gleamed a dark tan in the moonlight, and each of his arms bore feathered bands both at the biceps and at the wrists. He wore a brightly colored loincloth, cinched with a fur belt, probably monkey. His legs were muscled but bowed giving him a slightly comedic stance. Still, his stature was regal, and I assumed he was the chieftain of this band. Without speaking, he swiftly stretched forth his arm and impaled me with his spear, pushing it into my chest and holding me there. *"Mi Dios!"* I said.

My attacker simply stood there, looking at me with a passive curiosity. I saw the others rush toward my group of survivors and fall upon them viciously and without conscience, and then I could hear the screams and pleadings of the surprised, frightened, and tired men behind me. All the while, the one held me on my feet, impaled on his spear. The blood began to trickle out of my mouth.

"You came and disregarded our laws," said my attacker in Bisayâ, "by forcing on us a religion contrary to our own. For that, death." He steadied his end of the spear into the sand, thereby lifting me almost off my feet as I hung suspended in the night. I heard the last moans of those behind me, barely audible above the whispering tide. Having assured themselves that none of us would last the night, the natives left in silence.

As my life dimmed, the images of my nightmares came back, clearer and more vivid than ever before: it was never a dream of someone else's death but of my own, a violent death enacted upon me by others, faces I didn't know, and now, also faces I knew: Tomas and Efraim, Lydia. They were smiling. Were they smiling because I was dying? How had I disappointed them then? Or were they smiling with me? With some effort, I stretched my hand to press on my cilice, and then I also smiled. I knew the pleasure of heaven was soon going to follow this pain. And out of my mouth came the words I did not understand: "Finally, I can start anew."

Although no voice answered me, I heard the lifting of my soul from this useless shell, like a whisper of pleasure, rushing onward headlong to my destiny of delivering to others my gospel of pain.

Germany 1926-1945

Before I met Hitler, I was beset with night terrors, even into my twenties. They started when I was just a child when a lung inflammation kept me bedridden. In addition, I was cursed with a congenital deformity exacerbated by an occurrence of osteomyelitis. My right foot was twisted inward, and my right leg was weak and unformed, requiring a brace. My parents believed it a punishment from God for their misdeeds.

In childhood, I was terrified by my dreams – images of demons with twisted smiles reaching for me – from which I would awake startled and sweating. As I got older, the dreams, rather than diminishing, became more vivid. I no longer saw fanciful devils with horns and forked tails but rather, priests and their congregations dancing naked around night fires until they fell on one another with lustful appetites. At other times, I dreamt of pierced and shredded bodies lifeless on a tropical shore, seeming almost to tremble at the flow and ebb of a soft, green tide. No matter the content, I always awoke bathed in sweat and trembling.

By the time I finished my university studies, I considered myself a young radical utterly committed to national socialism, to the plight of the working classes, and to the return of Germany to its status as a European leader.

But in July 1925, when I heard Hitler speak, I became a different person. I, Joseph Goebbels, now knew that the man who led the Nazi Party was born to be our leader. I was ready to sacrifice everything for him, although I knew that in some details, Hitler's policies diverged from mine. Yet, his speech inspired me, and just as he ended his remarks with bright tears in his eyes for Germany, I was shaken by his devotion to his cause, so much so that I went outside afterward and stood by the window, crying like a baby. The National Socialist Party attracted me because of conditions and circumstances over which I had no control: my family was barely middle class, teetering in bad times on the edge of poverty; I was rejected from military service during the World War; and the aftermath of that war left much of Germany and its people in dire economic straits.

As an adult, I discovered that my only escape from my nightmares was when I was sleeping with a woman in bed beside me. It seemed to calm my mind and keep the night terrors at bay. Once I realized this, I seldom wanted for a woman in my bed. In short, I never needed anyone's pity although I used pity as an effective seduction.

Moreover, my various affairs with women of different backgrounds and classes provided me with the opportunity to see the importance of politics in one's life. Not my first, but one of my most significant relationships occurred when I was twenty-one and studying at Freiburg University. There I met Anka Stalherm, a beautiful twenty-one-year-old girl. It did not take me long to seduce her, but that seduction was fraught with problems.

"Surely you understand my position, Joseph," Anka pleaded a few months after our romance began. We were sitting on a bench in Möslepark surrounded by unkempt hedges.

"No, Anka, I cannot. You are telling me that you agree with your family's assessment of me. It is cruel to be recognized not for my intellect or spirit but, as your father says, 'a penniless cripple.' Is that why you sleep with me? Because you pity me?" I drew her closer to me.

Anka began to weep. "No, Joseph. It is cruel of you to say so. Have I not confessed how much I truly love you?"

"And yet you do as your mother wishes. You go to church to confess your relationship with me to be a sin for which you beg forgiveness. You light candles against me as if I were some demon." I blew softly in her ear, smiling as she thrilled in response.

"I only do so to satisfy my mother and father, not because I want to." She tried to pull away from me.

I gripped her closer. "Tell me you want me. Touch me, Anka. Kiss me."

"I do," she replied breathlessly.

Yet, despite her passion and my desire, we alternated between devotion and rejection. She could not help but realize that at university, I was merely tolerated, despite my intellectual acumen, because I lacked financial stability and depended on parents who, themselves, scraped and saved to stay solvent. The other students, including Anka, were stolidly middle-class, bourgeois capitalists who disdained people like me. It made me see myself as an outlaw of sorts, an enemy of capitalism and an advocate of socialism.

Anka and I were able, for a time, to overlook our differences because of our ardor. I offered a formal engagement, but she refused, upon which I offered to kill myself. Anka's promise of sincerity in her love for me kept me alive. Two years later, in 1920, I threatened suicide again because I could not afford to pay the fees needed to remain at the university; my father borrowed money to keep me at school. "You could have helped me by asking your parents to fund my studies," I said to Anka.

"They would have refused," she answered flatly. "Perhaps they would have even ordered me home, Joseph."

It didn't matter. Except for my affair with Anka, I was unhappy at Freiburg and transferred, with Anka, to Würzburg, but I ultimately decided to go alone to the University of Heidelberg, where I excelled, earning my Ph.D. in philology in 1921. I'd heard that Anka had left Würzburg shortly after me, married and divorced, and was living in Berlin. Without Anka, my night terrors resumed.

Now graduated and unemployed, I tried to break into publishing with two plays and a novel. Unsuccessful, I was forced to move to Cologne and take work in a bank, a job I hated. The nightmares, which had previously been visually vivid but audibly silent, now began to produce sound as well: anguished cries of pain, angry words of recrimination, and a disembodied voice that murmured calmly when the characters in my head were murdered, "Death at last."

I found that in my hometown of Rheydt, I could barely make a living among my own people, Germans. I started as a private tutor and did occasional work as a journalist for the local newspaper. I searched for a woman who could relieve my night terrors and found Else Janke, a local school teacher. While I was taking a walk one day, passing the local elementary school which I had, myself attended some twenty years before, I noticed a beautiful young woman with whom I immediately struck up a conversation. Certain that an alliance with her would banish my nightmares, I romanced her heavily; needless to add, I was sure that her charms would satisfy me sexually. Yet, she put me off, insisting on simply a friendship.

I was far more experienced, however, in matters of romance, and I knew that the way to win her consent was to play on her sympathies for me as a cripple. I complained to her about my life in general, my dissatisfaction with career opportunities, and my inability to find relief from the pain my deformed leg gave me. I shared with her my pessimism and the lack of empathy I found in most people. And then, I expressed to her my gratitude for her company.

"Else, you give me great comfort when I think of how kind you have been to listen to me all the time."

"Joseph, I do not pity you. I understand your feelings. Your disability has alienated you from the world. Yet, you are brilliant – you have earned a doctorate despite physical and economic struggles. I admire you greatly for your courage and your success."

I saw no limits to what I might do to ensure I had seduced a woman, bending her to my purpose. With Else, it was simply a matter of winning her concern for my well-being. So, I played heavily on her sympathies.

"I have a gift for you, Joseph, which I think will be of great assistance to you in lifting your spirits." She handed me a tissue-wrapped package.

She had given me a book of blank pages. "A journal?" I asked, turning the leather-bound volume in my hand.

"Yes, a diary. I think that it will help you to feel less negative about the world, as if in putting your darkest thoughts on paper, you are transferring the feelings outside of yourself, away from yourself, so they no longer give you pain." She smiled shyly.

"Thank you, Else. May I hug you?" I asked, leaning in towards her. She did not object when I embraced her. That first contact with her body inflamed me. I had to have her.

"I only hope it helps."

"Now, I need only wish for a miracle to release me from the constant reminder of my crippled leg. Unfortunately, no amount of writing can make that vanish."

Once I released her from my embrace, Else put her hand on my knee. "I will do what I can to relieve that as well," she answered, blushing.

"Oh, Else!" I exclaimed and swept her up in my arms. I whispered into her hair, "You are my true love!" and then I kissed her passionately, insisting with my lips and my tongue that she respond to me. "Gone the gentle Platonic love," I said, "and welcome to Eros, the sweeter passion."

When Else laughed, I knew she would be in my bed that very day; I'd found once again the way to keep my nightmares at bay. She was a timid lover at first, then responsive. As we settled in with one another, she became more interested in me.

"I read some of your opinions published in the newspaper, Joseph, and they bother me."

"What does, my dear?" I stretched out in bed beside her.

"You blame the Jews for so much," she explained.

"Not without reason," I answered. "They are a blight on our society." I loved Else but thought her naïve in many matters.

"I have some Jewish students who are quite bright and gentle," she answered.

I turned to her, leaning on an elbow, and smiled. "That is their way to insinuate themselves into our lives."

"You make it sound so evil, Joseph. Isn't it just assimilation?"

"You are a wonderful lover and, I'm sure, an admirable school teacher, but you have not studied politics or economics, my dear Else." I stroked her hair, her beautiful long neck.

"So, teach me, Joseph. Correct me if I am wrong." She leaned toward me, responding to my caresses.

I lay back and pulled her close to me, her head resting in the crook of my arm. "I have taught you to enjoy our love-making, no? Now, you want me to be *Herr doktor Goebbels* as well?" I laughed. "Okay, I will start with a question: what do you think of Communists?"

"They are loud and argumentative, always calling for change. Sometimes, they scare me because they seem to want nothing more than to overthrow the government."

"To replace it with what?" I asked.

Else hesitated. "I don't know. They don't always talk about what would come after their revolution."

"Yes, Else, you're right. As Nietzsche said, "Not free *from* what, but free *for* what? That is my point – they agitate for change but are quite mute about what will come after the change. I hate the Communists."

"I can sympathize with that, Joseph, but you have cleverly diverted our discussion from its original subject: your dislike of the Jews." Else chuckled. "I may not be so naïve as you think."

"Did you not know, Else, that most of the communists in Germany are, in fact, Jews? That the foremost communists – Lenin, Trotsky – are all Jews? Communism is their politics. They are one and the same." I shook my head in frustration. "And those who are not communists are capitalists, just as bad. Greedy bastards." I growled. "They engulf us."

"Joseph!" Else said, sitting up. "How much you simplify! It is too easy and too simple for you to equate one's politics with one's ethnicity. Surely, it is a fallacy that even I, a simple school teacher, can see."

"Sometimes, Else, what is most obvious is also most true. History has shown us that. We must ever be diligent against those who would destroy our civilization for their own benefit." I reached for her again. "Don't worry, my sweetheart, I will always protect you."

She snuggled against me once again and sighed. "I have to think about all of this, Joseph, and I would ask that you do the same. Their religion is Judaism, but they are Germans like us. We speak the same language, eat the same food, and raise our families the same. Their politics may be, as you say, destructive rather than constructive, but to what purpose for them? They would suffer just as we might under a poorly run government. Think about it, Joseph. They are unworthy of your scorn when you see how much they are just like us." She hugged me. "I don't wish to fight."

"Nor do I, Else," I said, kissing her neck. "No more talk," I said, putting a finger to her lips, "to spoil our sweet time together. You've given me a journal; I'll fill it with all the talk while I concentrate on making love to you."

Else and I carried on for two years, and we often talked about antisemitism, but we also had personal disagreements, reflecting our own insecurities about each other's true feelings, and financially, we were not earning enough to feel comfortable and secure.

Finally, one afternoon, while we sat by the river watching the swans float by, she said, "Joseph, we have talked about this many times, yet I've been unable to make you budge one inch from your position."

"It is because I am right about the Jews, Else. You see, all of Germany is waking up to the truth. The man who is sounding the alarm is gaining popularity and will one day, I predict, bring Germany back to its greatness by ridding us of all our enemies, especially the communist and capitalist Jews." I hugged her to me. "I heard him speak, Else. His name is Adolf Hitler. He is brilliant."

"Nothing I say seems to convince you," she said, "so I must now try with one last attempt." She drew even closer to me, pressing her head against my chest. One of the swans flapped his wings suddenly, disturbing the peace of the placid water. "I am a half-Jew," she whispered into my clothing.

For a moment, my arms around her felt numb. I caught my breath and stiffened. "You should not have kept this from me, Else." We were in a public park; I would not make a scene, although I felt betrayed. I was duped by this stupid school teacher of no consequence! I took her home and acted as if nothing were amiss, but I was already planning how I would cleverly extricate myself from this untenable relationship, which I managed when Hitler, impressed with my writing and public speaking skills, offered me the position of Berlin Gauleiter for the Nazi Party. I told Else I would be much too far away in Berlin for our relationship to continue.

Yet, I could not forget Else, even though I found another woman, Elisabeth Gensicke, to warm my bed while I was away from Else in Cologne. I enjoyed Else's devotion to me, and though I knew I couldn't ever marry her because she was a half-breed, I continued to meet with her irregularly. Once, by coincidence, I met with her best friend, Alma, and took up with her as well. Else, Elisabeth, Alma! They all pleased me, of course, but Anka!

On my way to Berlin to become one of Hitler's gauleiters that late October day in 1926, I smiled to be rid of the half-Jewess and thought with no small amount of regret how circumstances had conspired against me in my affair with Anka so many years earlier: she had been my true love, completely different from Else. Anka was quick-witted, clever, and intelligent; her family was pure Aryan, well-bred, and relatively wealthy. I had lost the perfect woman and did not think I would find another like her, But, five years later and after brief encounters with numerous women, I met and quickly married Magdalena "Magda" Behrend in 1931. Until then, I endured my night terrors heroically, for they had now incorporated both Else, the half-Jewess whose loyalty and industriousness attracted me, Elisabeth, who was older but reminded me of Anka, and Anka herself, for whom I harbored an unfulfilled longing. In those nightmares, all the women seemed to pull me apart, one representing a temptation for the forbidden, one smothering me with consolation, and the last teasing me with her unattainability.

My relief came finally because I had found Magda, who matched my love for the hero in my waking life, Adolf Hitler.

"It's not enough," I said bitterly. "I will be thirty-six this year and not getting any younger."

"You've been a fool to think he would simply drop it in your lap," Magda said to me, leaning closer to stroke my thigh. "He is testing you, that's all."

"It's not fair. I have been devoted to him for nearly ten years, since 1924, and he rewards me with crumbs, Magda. Tell me, dear wife, what must I do to be made a Reich Minister?" I pushed her hand away and leaned forward. "Don't touch my leg."

"First, do not rebuff my affections," she commanded, pointedly stroking my face. "Next, do what he says without question - keep that appointment with Hanussen."

I lost my patience. "When you touch this leg," I said, lifting the trouser to reveal the brace beneath it, "you remind me that I am a cripple. I have already told you that I do not like that." I thought Magda was sometimes insensitive; her beautiful, pure Aryan looks – blond hair, fair skin, blue eyes – seemed to assert an unfounded superiority over my more ordinary appearance of dark hair and eyes and short stature.

I gripped her wrist, pulling it away from my face. "And Hanussen is a Jew. Why should I see him?" When I saw Magda wince because I was squeezing her hand too hard, I pulled it closer and kissed it softly. "Please, Magda, let us remember that our marriage must be outwardly happy at Adolf's insistence. We need only *look like* the perfect couple of the National Socialist Party." I dropped her hand. "I will go see this Hanussen tomorrow as scheduled, but it will be a waste of my time."

Magda and I had once been happy, but our marriage proved that it was our deep devotion to Hitler that kept us together, not love for one another. She was beautiful and sexy, and I was the envy of many of my colleagues, but she basked in the attention of all men, especially Adolf's. In fact, she spent much of her time with him while I worked to boost his public image. It was Adolf, in fact, who constantly referred to us as "the perfect Reich couple." Implied in his compliment was the suggestion that if we truly loved him, we would not disappoint him.

"Joseph," Magda said, sighing loudly, "just go. Tonight, we must present ourselves as the most faithful and happiest followers of Adolf, knowing that he will soon realize that your efforts were instrumental in his appointment as Chancellor of Germany. Have you arranged the parade?"

"For tonight? Of course. Berlin will glow with the lights of sixty thousand torches marching through the streets, many in the SS and the SA. I have ordered every house to be adorned with our banner. Adolf is bound to be impressed."

Magda replied, "I'm glad for Heinrich Himmler's *Schutzstaffel*; his Protection Squads are disciplined and trustworthy, but Ernst Röhm's *Sturmabteilung*! They call themselves Storm Troopers as if they were elite, but they are nothing more than thugs in their brown shirts and jackboots."

"All serve their purpose, Magda. Do you not see that the SS are there for the German people to admire and take pride in, while the SA are there to persuade and convince them to join our ranks or suffer consequences? We leave nothing to chance." I leaned down and adjusted the brace on my withered leg. "I need my cocaine powder. Where is it?"

"I'll fetch it from the kitchen cabinet," Magda offered. "Would you like a whiskey with that?" She rose from the couch.

"No, I need to be alert tonight."

Once the parade started, I installed Magda on the reviewing stand with Hermann Göring, the Minister of Aviation, who was to give the keynote speech. Magda's job was to stay close to Adolf, making sure he was satisfied with the spectacle. I went backstage to review the parade route and schedule and to make sure that Göring's speech was being broadcast live on the radio.

This was another of my achievements for Adolf and the

Nazi party: I had used what I termed my policy of *überreden und drohen* – to persuade and to threaten – in order to assure that all of Germany's radio stations would broadcast the parade live, as it was happening, rather than hear someone's second-hard description of it afterwards. The listeners would hear the resounding cheers, the sounds of marching boots on the cobble-stone streets and the crackling fires of thousands of torches. They would hear Göring's enthusiasm for Hitler's chancellor-ship and be convinced it was destiny because Göring was the nation's hero of World War One despite the fact that he had grown fat and conceited these last two years. I left nothing to chance, especially because I was aware of how easily we could fail if we allowed dissent.

At the end of the night, Magda came backstage with Adolf on her arm. "He was asking after Helga," she said to me.

Smiling and bowing to Adolph, I said, "Your goddaugh-ter is asleep in bed as any good child of ours should be at this hour." It was after midnight.

"You two must take good care of her and, in fact, give her many siblings," Adolf said, patting Magda's hand and nodding at me.

"Of course, Chancellor," Magda said, "we are hard at work to assure your adopted family grows quickly."

I nodded in agreement. In fact, Magda and I had already decided, after two years of marriage, that what we most had in common was our admiration for Hitler and our belief that he alone would restore Germany to greatness after its ignominious defeat in World War One. In addition, we realized that we pre-ferred the company of others rather than of one another.

In my position as one of Adolf's trusted advisors, my forte was in dealing with the media – newspapers and radio, and even the arts, graphic, theatrical, musical, and literary. So, I found myself among creative people, many of them attractive women whose charms I enjoyed; some were attracted to me by dint of my position or my personality, and those who weren't could be easily "convinced." Besides, I had long suspected that

Magda and Adolf enjoyed a sexual relationship, although I could never prove it. Nor did I care to because we had reputations to protect. We would couple to produce children but find our pleasures elsewhere.

Adolf treated us as family, often making sure to take pictures with us and Helga; to her, he was "Uncle Adolf," the beaming, solicitous relative who always had candy or a kind word for her. Magda and I understood that this relationship was all that Adolf allowed himself because he had dedicated himself to a greater cause: Germany's return to its position of power on the European continent and, eventually, its total conquest of the world. He was sacrificing a personal life for his country!

"So," Adolf asked, "have you seen Hanussen yet?" He squinted at me.

"The appointment is tomorrow, Adolf. Uh – *Herr Kanzler*." I corrected myself, using his new title of Chancellor. I saw the grin spread on his face, and he puffed out his chest in pleasure.

"You will not be disappointed," he said. Turning to Magda, he brushed her cheek with a kiss and said, "Take care of this fellow, will you, dear?"

Magda laughed lightly and nodded. "I will, of course, because I – *we* – love you dearly and know you have only our best interests at heart. If you say that Hanussen is clairvoyant, then Joseph will surely want to know what is in store for the Goebbels family in the coming years."

When we arrived home, I said to Magda, "I'm telling you, Hanussen's a conniving Jew. What use could he possibly be to me?" Magda knew and shared my misgivings about Jews: I was certain that their prominent place in publishing had prevented me from becoming a celebrated author of fiction and that their politics were aligned with Marxist communism and the hateful Russian Lenin. Finally, everyone knew that they, as bankers and financiers, were the source of Germany's economic collapse in 1930. They had insinuated themselves into German society as if they were Germans rather than Jews, and they diluted our culture.

"Adolf knows he is a Jew, but he says that, nevertheless, he is a brilliant clairvoyant. Adolf wants you to subject yourself to him to learn your future; Hanussen's usefulness will wear itself out, I'm sure, but for now, just humor Adolf."

I knew Magda well enough to realize that she was a shrewd observer of character. Although Adolf was often unreadable and contradictory, to Magda, he was predictable or malleable. She knew, better than I when to yield to Adolf's demands and when to subtly alter them to her own purposes. I admired that about her.

That night, we coupled; it was purposeful but without passion. And when we finished, I retired to my own bedroom, carrying my clumsy steel brace as I limped silently down the hall. As I lay in bed, drifting in twilight sleep, I recalled some of my tragic childhood.

"Mama, mama, it hurts so much. Please, mama!" I begged.

"*Still, mein Kind*" – Hush, my child, my mother responded, leaning forward to stroke my forehead. "The fever will pass, and you will no longer feel any pain."

But she didn't know what she was talking about, my poor, dumb, dear Mother. My pain was real, almost unbearable for a nine-year-old child who wanted only to stop hurting. The muscles in my right leg constantly cramped, as if some unseen gargantuan hand were squeezing them. Fever soaked my body in hot-then-cold sweat until my skin recoiled from any touch, even that of the thin sheet and the nightshirt covering me. I thrashed about in my narrow bed as if to shake off the aching of my limbs. What had I done, I wondered, to be treated so cruelly by God?

Two days later, after the fever broke and I finally slept, exhausted, through the night, I got out of bed only to find that my right foot was twisted inward and the entire length of the leg stiff. I hobbled to the mirror in my parents' bedroom and looked: I was pale and sallow, my hair stood in unwieldy cowlicks from the fever, and I was noticeably tilted to the right as I was leaning heavily on my right leg.

"Paul Joseph!" my mother exclaimed from the doorway. "You should not be out of bed."

"I am even more useless now than before," I said to her reflection in the mirror. Then, I started to cough uncontrollably, my lungs betraying their inability to provide me with constant regular breaths. My shriveled leg added disfigurement to my already diagnosed weak respiratory system.

"Unsinn! Geh wider ins Bett und ruhe dich aus." – Nonsense! Go back to bed and rest. She moved forward to grasp my shoulders and turn me away from the mirror. *"Morgan wird es dir gut gehen.* – Tomorrow, you will be fine. – We will all learn to live with this punishment from God." She marched me back to my room and tucked me in, even though it was a beautiful summer morning, and the sun was shining.

I lay passively in my bed. I could hear my older brothers, Konrad and Hans, playing outside. I closed my eyes. I would never be fine.

Erik Jan Hanussen, I knew, was the alias of Hershmann-Chaim Steinschneider, the son of a Jewish itinerant performer in Vienna. After years as a showman in various circuses and cabarets, the young man adopted the identity of a noble Scandinavian (thus, *Erik Jan Hanussen*) as a clairvoyant. When he settled in Berlin, he rode on the wave of the popularity of the occult, and soon drew the interest of various Nazi officials who recommended him to Hitler.

I was far more educated than many of my colleagues, so I knew that Hanussen's so-called clairvoyance was little more than his shrewd manipulation of the tools of astrology, parapsychology, and street smarts. I was determined to pay him nothing more than lip service, and then report back to Adolf that my meeting was "instructive."

I met him at his opulent apartment in Berlin, which he called "The Palace of the Occult." He entertained not only the elite of Berlin society, but also various high-level Nazi officials; he clearly enjoyed establishing relationships with those in power. "We have much to discuss," he said without a smile. "Much."

"I will not lie. I think you a charlatan, and I am here only because the man I admire above all others, Adolf Hitler, has insisted I speak with you." I refused his handshake and seated myself on his sofa without his invitation.

"Then, we shall treat this as a strictly business meeting to avoid any interpretation of friendship, eh?" Hanussen said amiably.

"As you wish. I intend to spend as little time with you as possible," I declared, wanting to add *because you are a Jew*, but my upbringing as a decent Christian prevented me from such rude and brutal honesty.

"You may learn something from us Jews after all," he answered and shrugged.

At first I was shocked that he seemed to know what I was thinking, but then I laughed. "So you know that I have already investigated you."

"No more than I have investigated you, Joseph Goebbels." He lit a cigarette. "You know what they say in the cabarets of Berlin, *Herr Doktor*? They joke that a good Aryan Nazi is as blond as Hitler, as thin as Göring, and as chaste as you. But that is only jest, is it not?" He smiled and leaned back. "Before I tell you about your future, you must tell me something of your past."

"I'm not sure I want to share that information with you," I answered. I determined that the joke about Hitler, Göring, and me would not go unpunished.

"Then we will have to tell Herr Hitler that you were not cooperative." He sneered.

The threat was empty as far as I was concerned. I could

spin my own tale of how the meeting had failed, I was sure. "Do not threaten me, Hanussen."

"No threats, just observations and questions. Are you afraid of being hypnotized? Of your own subconsciousness?"

A challenge? I thought. I had never been hypnotized, although I was curious about the process. I'd read that only the weak of mind were susceptible, and that surely was not me. "More trickery. And how would you prove what I'd said while hypnotized?"

"Have you heard of sounding paper? An invention of a compatriot of mine, an Austrian, named Fritz Pfleumer. It will record what you say and play it back on his companion invention, a device called a tape recorder. However, I can only record a very small portion of what you say."

I was momentarily fascinated by this new invention, thinking immediately of its usefulness to the medium of radio. But, to Hanussen's point: "Then it sounds useless until it is better developed."

"Ah, but you clearly did not know that what you say under hypnosis is not forgotten by you once I bring you back, so to speak. You will remember it all."

I hesitated, tempted. Then, "Tell me again, what is the purpose of this hypnosis?"

"We are both artists, Goebbels; don't you remember Shakespeare who said, 'What's past is prologue'? It will propel us into the future."

"Understand this: I believe this will be your unmasking, your Norwegian persona stripped off to show the Viennese Jew underneath."

"Perhaps you might also have a mask that will fall?" he shrugged. He turned off all his lights, drew closed his heavy brocaded drapes, and told me to stretch out on his couch. He wheeled in a cart on which was a metal box with film reels and, beside it, a microphone like those used in radio transmissions. He stood above me at the head of the sofa. "Just focus on the light." About three feet above my head, he held a flashlight, which he clicked on and off. "And relax while you travel back."

"*Mi dios!*" I shouted, the Spanish words strange in my mouth.

"What do you see? Where are you?" Hanussen asked calmly.

"I am impaled on a spear. I am on a shore in a tropical place. I am wearing monk's robes. I am dying." It was a movie that I was both starring in and watching as a member of the audience.

"Go back earlier. Relax."

I reached into my head as if I were plucking a flower from a field filled with flowers. "I am being pulled apart, limb from limb, in a cold harbor. There is blood and many grasping hands. I am dying."

But there was no pain, only the unspooling of the vision as if I were both participant and observer, victim and murderer.

"Go back earlier. Relax."

"I am blank. There is only whiteness. Incoherent whispers." I was suddenly weary.

"Wake up. Remember everything."

When I sat up, I rubbed my chest where the spear had pierced me and my arms, which had been torn from their sockets. "What was that?" I asked, whispering.

"Past lives. You have seen your past lives," Hanussen said. "It is an Asian belief that we live successive lives until we finally achieve Paradise when we have corrected the wrongs we have committed." He spoke authoritatively, as if instructing me.

"Anamnesis. That is what you're talking about. That I've lived before."

"You've studied Asian religions?" Hanussen seemed suddenly hesitant. I saw in his eyes the realization that I was more learned than he, that I was *authentic* and he was no more than a fake.

"I've studied linguistics. Language informs everything, including religion."

"I don't understand," Hanussen said. "I don't understand the connection, but more, I don't understand what just happened." Hanussen was a mere charlatan, so this turn of events frightened him. He could neither control the situation nor me.

I was less fearful than curious. "I swear you to secrecy on this, Hanussen, or I will make your life incredibly difficult. Until I get to the bottom of this, we will meet regularly, and we will unravel the mystery of my revelations. Do you understand?"

"Goebbels, you cannot force me to help you in this. There is something unholy in this." His voice trembled.

I watched the man Hanussen become fearful of having faced the unknown; he was smaller and weaker, superstitious, without confidence. As far as I was concerned, it was the true nature of the Jew revealed: subhuman. I cleared my throat. "I will say only this. Within a year, our Party will be dominant in Germany. The Weimar Republic will fall, and a new, nationalist Germany will rise. Trust me on this: Adolf Hitler's dream of a pure Aryan Germany will come true. I am the clairvoyant in this, not you. Do you understand?"

"Please, Herr Goebbels, this is unearthly. I will find someone else to hypnotize you, to help you."

"We have opened the door together. I will have no one else with us in this." I shook my head. "And if you should falter, I will remind you that we are building a place in Dachau where we will lock up all who oppose us, all who would threaten our success. So, I require your continued assistance and silence."

Hanussen nodded meekly.

When Magda asked me about the meeting, I laughed cynically. "I have lived before, Magda!" I explained, "I have discovered that this is not my only life, but it will be my *best* life. There will be no limits on me, no restrictions. I shall, as I did before, revel in excess."

"And what of Adolf?" Magda asked.

"He is the star to which I attach myself, my dear. What brilliance shines from him has been cultivated by me. I am the power behind the throne. I will serve him until the time comes when I might replace him. Everything in due time." My night-mares had been altered: still frightening and violent but now also somehow delicious and satisfying.

The Unraveling

I told Adolf that Hanussen had seen me playing a role in Germany's renaissance under Hitler's leadership, and while I believed this to be true, only a single word in that assertion did Hanussen actually speak: *renaissance*. And even that he had spoken hesitantly.

"I would more accurately call it *rebirth*, Goebbels," he corrected himself. "Renaissance implies renewal; the other, rebirth, more probably infers replication."

We'd been meeting regularly for two months and, with hypnosis, had fleshed out some of the contents of my two previous lives. When apart, we studied texts and spoke to scholars about the concept of reincarnation. In my own time, I began research on what little information I had about the characters in my dreams. I discovered only a single reference, the Lanercost Chronicle, to the Scottish priest of my dreams: he was unnamed but killed by a Christian mob after he led young women in a dance to Dionysus; as for the Spanish friar also in those dreams, I could only surmise from my studies that he was probably one of the first Augustinian friars who did missionary work in the Philippines. So, they were real, I thought. But why were they in my dreams for so many years, torturing me with their pain and unusual deeds? There was no connection to me, I thought, and my research led me only to references to Dionysus, who I began to read about in earnest. "Yes, I agree that my present life seems to be developing more along the lines of replication. It's a more probable explanation."

"And what do you think is being replicated?" Hanussen asked. He had become less fearful of our discovery and more interested in learning its details.

I shook my head. "I'm not sure." I did not hate the man any less. In fact, I hated him more because he had learned something about me which I considered highly personal and confidential. There were too many ambitious people around me who might use such information against me. So, I shared as little as possible with Hanussen. In fact, I had already set in motion my plan to ensure Hanussen's silence.

"If I may be so bold, Goebbels, you should see that your current reincarnation is a perfect opportunity to ensure it is your last. That is, if you use this life to atone on your death, you will enter into eternal Paradise, your just reward." He smiled.

"Yes, it would require, of course, that I acknowledge the errors of my past lives in order to atone for them in this life, right?" I asked ironically.

Hanussen hesitated then agreed, oblivious to my irony. "Yes, yes. I think you should see your present successes as foretastes of Paradise if you renounce and correct all that has been done in previous lives."

"Indeed, there have been successes after all," I agreed. "As far back as December 1930, I was instrumental in creating German opposition to the showing of that American film *All Quiet On The Western Front,* which depicted us as pitiful losers. The National Socialists, our party under Hitler, sought to revive pride in German culture. We boycotted the theaters and made the film's distribution in Germany a failure.

"Then, that torchlight parade in January 1933 convinced much of Germany that Hitler was the man to trust. And, in February, when the Communists set the Reichstag, our hallowed Senate building, afire, we were able to crush them by pressuring von Hindenburg to sign the Fire Decree."

"Was it, indeed, necessary?" Hanussen asked quietly.

I grinned. "Be careful, Hanussen. I know you have always sympathized with those liberal freedoms that are the curse of democratic governments. But I saw that to unify and strengthen Germany, we had to temporarily suspend free speech, free assembly, and even a free press."

He sighed. "Think carefully. Every act has consequences." I marked his overt criticism as yet another of his stupidities.

I ignored him. "Then, the Senate passed the Enabling

Act, giving Hitler complete power. And now that I have finally been appointed to Hitler's cabinet as Reich Minister of Propaganda, you will see that I can do so much more to restore Germany to its position of superiority in Europe."

"My clairvoyance is pointless these days; everyone sees where Germany is headed. Besides, I have been more involved with discovering your past, Goebbels." He was clumsily making a case for his innocence; he did not want me to think him dangerous to me.

"And thanks for all your efforts," I said. "I release you from service now. Despite your admonitions, be certain that you may request anything of me that you need." I rose to gather my coat and hat and shake Hanussen's hand.

The following week, the last in March, I was told that Hanussen was found dead in his apartment, a small box stuffed with IOUs from various Nazi officers at his bedside. The informant who had sent the police to his apartment had convincingly implicated Hanussen in the Reichstag Fire.

By this time, Hitler had lost interest in the man and in clairvoyance itself, insisting that only what science could prove was true; all else was deception and deceit. I spoke to no one about Reincarnation except to Magda, who said its mysticism aroused her sexual interest in me, and so our promise to Hitler to produce brothers and sisters for our daughter was renewed with some vigor. When I recounted events of my past lives to her, she would sometimes suggest that we try to recreate them ourselves, from sexual excesses to physical injuries. Others would have called our role-playing perversions; we understood them to be expressions of power and control. Surely, despite Hanussen's conclusions, there was nothing I needed to be forgiven for.

The Ministry of Propaganda, formally called the Ministry for Public Enlightenment and Propaganda, was moved into an eighteenth-century palace across from Hitler's Chancellery. I made sure that it gathered under its umbrella the functions of other, lesser ministries, the point being to centralize my control of all aspects of German cultural and intellectual life and of mass media. Although assigned only about three hundred employees, I intended the Ministry to grow exponentially by establishing not only departments of administration, propaganda, broadcasting, press, film, and the arts (theater, music, literature and art) but also a department of security which would guard against lies at home and abroad and be responsible for tourism. Thus, I had at hand the power to control almost all aspects of the ordinary German's life.

"We must demonstrate our authority," I told my colleague, Heinrich Himmler, explaining my rationale for the proposed boycott of Jewish businesses.

"It is not the responsibility of the SS to stand guard over commercial enterprises," Himmler responded. We two were naturally suspicious of one another: both highly educated and organized, and both sickly in childhood. Our similarities should have united us against some of the others in Hitler's cabinet – big, sturdy, healthy men who were at ease in social circumstances – but we instinctively knew that our similarities marked us as competitors for Hitler's approval.

"It is your opportunity to show that the SS is a valuable force and should be the preeminent Nazi military over Erich Röhm's gang of SA bullies. I tell you, Heinrich, you should not allow the opportunity to pass you by."

Himmler slid his bookish glasses down his nose and looked at me over the rims. "Perhaps. But you must let me decide their on-site behavior."

He had overseen the design of Dachau, a modern detention center for political enemies of the National Socialists. It utilized isolation, punishing labor, and harsh, exacting obedience; Hitler approved it as a model for future concentration camps throughout Germany. Himmler loved detail, much like me, and whatever he planned, I knew would give the boycott significance. "Yes, I agree." We both stood and shook hands.

I publicized the economic boycott of Jewish businesses

and offices on April 1, 1933. I made sure to present it to the German people (through radio and newspapers) as reprisal for the Jews, both German and foreign, who were spreading rumors that damaged Germany's reputation in the international community. It was to be a one-day embargo on the Jews, meant not so much to hurt their business as much as to show how easily we could control some aspect of their lives.

Himmler, I was delighted to see, outdid himself. I visited the Wertheim Department Store, the largest in Berlin, and noted that it had closed and locked its doors. There were customers outside insisting the store be opened, but to no avail. Wertheim had been frightened into closing.

I then went to the Tietz department store. It, too, was closed, the iron grates drawn locked at its façade. Himmler's soldiers stood silently in front of signs they had posted: "Germans, defend yourselves against Jewish propaganda and only buy at German shops." At smaller establishments, the SS chased potential customers away by refusing to move from doorways or by asking passersby, "Will you support the homeland?" I strolled down one of the commercial streets and saw posts on numerous shops: "This shop closed by the police because of price gouging. Proprietor in custody in Dachau." It was signed "The Commander of the Political Police, Himmler." I ordered my assistant to find a cameraman to take a picture of this last sign; I wanted to memorialize it in my diary.

Less than a week later, I was notified that the Nazi German Student Association of the Humboldt University Law School in Berlin was preparing a press release of some importance. I called the main office to speak with the chapter president, Gunther.

"What are you up to, my young friend," I asked amiably.

"Something you will like, Herr Doktor Goebbels." He was a courteous fellow.

"*Sag es mir bitte* – Tell me, please."

"We are working on some statements to declare our allegiance to the Fürher, and we will present these at some evening event we have not yet determined."

I thought a moment. "So, your statements will be reminiscent of Luther's 95 Theses, which declared his displeasure with the Church?"

"Ah, that's a wonderful comparison we had not imagined. Thank you, Herr Doktor. Will you help us fashion the statement?"

"I would rather it was more naturally expressed as you students see fit. But, be sure to emphasize the need for purifying German language and literature, excised of Jewish intellectualism. You might want to demand that universities be the centers of German nationalism. And be sure to remind your audience that this is all in response to the international Jewish smear campaign against us Germans." My experience told me that lies asserted as truths can be accepted as truth in the hands of skilled orators and propagandists.

"I have written it all down, and our group will work on it. We plan on creating a press release and supply it to Association chapters throughout Germany. Perhaps we should also prepare a blacklist of un-German authors as well?"

I laughed. "You are in luck, young man. My office has been compiling just such a list for some time now; I'll send you copies immediately. And what event are you planning? When?"

"It will take some time, so we're aiming for early May. We thought, perhaps, a candlelight vigil?"

"May is good – your classes will be winding down a bit. But, a vigil is too passive. You are young people – demonstrate your enthusiasm, your welcoming of a new way of life. May I suggest something?"

"I would be honored if you would," Gunther answered eagerly.

"Line up some speakers, some well-known Nazi speakers who can inspire crowds. Have all the chapters negotiate with radio stations for airtime. And, best of all, show your revolutionary spirit by breaking with the old: have a *Säuberung durch*

Feuer – a clean sweep by fire."

Gunther asked, "Like a bonfire?"

"Yes, yes. Are you familiar with the bonfires of the Italian monk Savonarola of Florence? He called them 'bonfires of the vanities,' in which he advocated the destruction of secular art and culture. Similarly, you should burn something significant, something associated with learning." I was enjoying leading this young mind.

"I'm sorry. I don't understand."

"You must study your history more closely, Gunther. Where did Luther flee after posting his theses and being excommunicated?"

"Thuringia, if I recall correctly."

"And what is that otherwise ordinary place known for because of university students?"

"I am ashamed to say I do not know." Gunther sounded crestfallen.

"It was the only other event to promote German nationalism at a time when our country was nothing more than a scattered mix of independent states: the students held a burning of texts and literature they determined to be un-German."

"Ah!" Gunther sighed. "*Wunderbar!*"

"All right. Get to work, my young friend, and let me know when the event is set. I will broadcast it, of course."

"Will you attend?" Gunther asked hopefully.

"I'm sorry, my schedule does not permit it," I answered. In fact, I worried that an announcement of my attendance might lead someone to look into my academic background and discover that I had, as a student, aligned myself with some of my Jewish professors.

I hung up and looked out of my window across the way to the building that housed Hitler's chancellery. It had originally been the city palace of a prince, then the chancellery of all of Germany's governors. Hitler wanted a different place, one not associated with the old regimes. I imagined this chancellery going up in flames and noted to myself that our party, the National Socialists, seemed to be symbolized, in part, by fire icons: torchlight parades, the burning of the Reichstag that ushered us into power, and now a book burning.

That night, sitting with Magda in our apartment, I asked, "When is the child due?"

She patted her still-flat belly. "I think January or February of next year, Joseph."

"I am hoping for another daughter." I laid my head on her stomach.

"Not a son?" Magda asked, surprised.

"I still fear I will pass on my infirmity, this blasted twisted foot."

"That's not how it works, Joseph."

"Not how what works?" The mantle clock struck ten.

"Reincarnation. Characteristics are passed from one life to another, not from parent to child. So, your Scottish priest had a clubfoot and a lazy eye. Your Spanish friar had a single testicle. And you have your twisted foot and respiratory problems."

"So I need not worry that my child will also be deformed? That is comforting if true. Do you think, then, that our attitudes and proclivities are part of our reincarnations?"

Magda laughed. "Is it not already true, Joseph? You have sexual appetites that, at their most normal, are just an excessive number of affairs with women, but at their most perverse is the bloodlust you have for the complete annihilation of Jews."

"That is not sexual, Magda," I protested.

"Isn't it? You can't tell me you aren't aroused – and satisfied – with every idea and action that is detrimental to the Jews. The Scots priest in you wanted to sexually debase everyone he knew; the Spanish friar in you wanted to give and feel the pain that was so intense it became a pleasure. The German Aryan in you wants the power and control to assert your will over everyone except your God." Magda leaned down and bit my lip until I tasted a drop of blood on my tongue.

"That hurt, Magda."

"And then?"

"And then it felt good. Or was it just good when you let go of my lip?"

"It doesn't matter, Joseph. Pain will always lead to pleasure." She laid my hand on her breast. "Will you do the same for me?"

I squeezed her breast until she winced, and I did not let go until she gasped and then smiled. "There are many ways I can hurt you, Magda, besides physically."

"You have taught me to enjoy it all. And," she added, reaching under my head to retrieve something from the pocket of her dress, "I have a gift for you." She produced a shiny metal coin, irregular instead of perfectly round.

"What is it?" I asked, peering at it as I held it up in the air. There was barely an outline of a face on one side, but unrecognizable because it had worn away. On the reverse was a rough imprint of a cross.

"I was told by the antiquarian who obtained it for me that it is a coin from Attica, Greece, from about 60 A.D. He thinks it was struck to commemorate the assimilation of two religious forces at play: the older worship of Dionysus and the newer introduction of Catholicism by St. Paul, thus the face on one side and the cross on the other. Do you like it?"

I turned it over in my hand, catching a glint of light. "I am touched, Magda, that you remember my Scottish incarnation as a disciple of Dionysus."

"And your Spanish one as a disciple of Christ."

I tightened my fist around the coin. "I will cherish this and remain a Catholic."

"Why?" Magda asked, astonished at the revelation.

"Adolf has insisted I do so. He says it is for tactical reasons."

"In other words, he understands that we must not seem hostile to the Church at this point."

"Yes. And how easy it will be for me to do this for him, Magda. I am, after all, the inheritor of both a priest and a friar!" I grunted. "In fact, I once actually wanted to be a priest!"

"He will see one day, Joseph, that you and I are his most devoted friends."

"There is much to do before then."

Purifying Fire

On April 8th, newspapers published the students' "Twelve Theses", which promoted "action against the un-German spirit." The statement ended with an invitation to the *Säuberung durch Feuer* – cleansing by fire – to be held two days hence at Opera Square in Berlin and simultaneously at more than thirty other university towns throughout Germany.

The Square itself was a large open space almost completely surrounded by eighteenth-century buildings: the Opera House, St. Hedwig's Cathedral, the Old Library Building, the Palace of Fredrick the Second's brother, and the main building of Humboldt University. Four days prior to the announced Cleansing, the nationalist German Student Association forcibly ransacked the Institute for the Science of Sexuality; the institute's records and some twenty thousand of its library books, unique works on sexuality topics, were dragged to the Square for burning.

I arrived around nine p.m., surprising the crowd of forty thousand people who had initially been informed that I would not appear. I waited in my car while a table and microphones were prepared for me. I was pleased to see not only SA and SS soldiers in uniform, but also students, professors, and ordinary citizens crowding together, cheering on student speakers and those who were building and feeding the bonfire structure that illuminated the square.

"Make sure that the burnings continue during my speech," I ordered. Surrounded by men of both the SA and the SS in their brown or black uniforms, I wore only an ordinary suit under my raincoat, and I removed my swastika armband, shoving it surreptitiously into my pocket. I wanted the crowd to focus on my voice and my words, not my appearance.

To that end, I made sure the dais was not more than a foot off the ground. On it was set a simple table covered with a cloth bearing the swastika and, in front, were the microphones for transmission to radios throughout Germany. The dais itself faced the bonfire but was set about fifty feet away, placing some of the crowd between the fire and the podium. Its light would be reflected on my face as I spoke, as if I were, myself, on fire with fervor.

Students had been speaking for about an hour before I arrived, and between speeches, the crowds sang nationalist songs, cheered each time the bonfire was fed an armload of books, and enthusiastically saluted the entrance or exit of each speaker. I was gratified but not surprised by the roar of the audience when my name was announced.

I waited dramatically for the cheers to die down, so all we heard was the sound of papers crackling in the fire. Tiny embers and ash floated in the dark, cool Spring night. When I was assured that I had their attention, I spoke. "Jewish intellectualism is dead," I began, raising my fist in the air. With each statement, the crowd expressed its agreement. Like background music, there was the steady thud of books being tossed into the fire and the sharp crackle of bindings and pages curling into ash, counterpoints to my words. "The old goes up in flames," I explained and paused. Then, "The new shall rise from the ashes." I was invoking the legend of the phoenix to illustrate a new Germany on the horizon.

But my ardor that night was not only for my Fatherland but for myself, also risen from the remnants of my past lives. It was not just a rebirth, not just coming back. It was my life fashioned from previous ones, but *better*. I watched the flames consume those books – at least twenty thousand volumes, I later learned – and I understood that this was symbolic of a shedding of my own immediate past as a mediocre cripple German bourgeoisie. I was becoming a strong, powerful Aryan of the future, second only to my leader – *mein Führer* – Adolf Hitler. In my pocket, I clutched the ancient coin.

I felt the passion of the Scots Malcolm filling me, the zeal of the Spaniard Diego, giving my voice strength and conviction. What they had attained in their lives came rushing into me, a power immense enough to govern a nation. At that moment, the bonfire lighting my face, I knew that, except for Hitler's greatness and brilliance, I could lead Germany! Only when the knee of my crippled leg buckled and I almost fell, did I feel the pain of Malcolm's flesh being torn to pieces and Diego's lungs filling with fatal blood; it was ecstasy!

To applause and exhortations, I retired to my car, instructing the driver to stay a few moments so we could listen to the crowd singing the Horst-Wessel song and watch some of the SA and SS march smartly in columns around the square. I massaged my leg where the brace had rubbed against it. Yet, that pain was nothing compared to the excitement I felt at this rally; my face still felt warm from the burning fires, and my ears rang with the voices chanting and singing in the square.

When I arrived home, I was exhausted yet exhilarated by the experience and woke Magda by embracing her roughly. Although I knew it would bruise her, I did not remove my leg brace. Before she was fully awake, I forced myself onto her until she surrendered meekly to my advances.

The next morning, I sat in the window to write in my journal. Magda lay sleeping quietly, small bites and bruises on her body, evidence of my dominance of her last night. I thought about the *Säuberung* and then wrote:

> May 11. Worked until late at
> home. In the evening, I gave
> a speech outside the opera
> house, in front of the bonfire,
> while the filthy, trashy books
> were being burned by the
> students. I was at the top of
> my form. Huge crowds. Su-
> perb summer weather began
> today.

The month of May was glorious for me, particularly in my goal to further discredit and alienate the Jews. At the start of the month, I coordinated the media announcements that "exposed" the Communist infiltration of the trade unions. By midmonth, despite some complaining, the government had dismantled the unions, appropriated all their funds, and imprisoned most of their leaders, even those who insisted they agreed with our politics. As Hitler's cabinet, all of us agreed that the unions had to be nationalized.

Then, I began plans for the Fifth Party Congress to take place in Nurenberg from August 30th to September 3rd. Hitler himself told me to contact a filmmaker he liked, Leni Riefenstahl, to discuss filming the event. I put off contacting her because I was trying to convince Thomas Mann, who had won the Nobel Prize in 1929, to return to Germany. At first, he refused to talk to me; when he did – on the telephone, from his self-imposed exile in Switzerland – he was contemptuous.

"But, *Herr* Mann, you must understand that your political writings, being contrary to our political philosophies, had to be banned for the sake of solidarity in Germany. Your body of fiction remains available to and beloved by the public." Surely, I thought, he would not desert the country that had nurtured him despite some differences of opinion.

"You have already exiled writers who I admire. You burn books – do you hear me? – *you burn books*. Would you deprive Germany of the knowledge of Einstein, Brecht, Hesse, and even Kafka? You are scoundrels and, worse, monsters." Mann muttered.

"Would you not agree that literature is merely a matter of taste?"

"To develop taste, one must be given choices." He sounded exasperated.

I had no time to continue such academic discussions with him; I lost my temper. "If you continue to refuse our offer of friendship, I'm afraid you might find yourself stripped of your citizenship and all your honors rescinded."

Mann sighed. "*Wenn das sein muss, akzeptiere ich es –* If that is what must be, I accept it." He hung up the phone so softly that I was, for a moment, not even sure we had been disconnected. I shrugged and turned my attention to the prospective filmmaker of the rally.

When I met Leni Riefenstahl, I thought her the very paragon of German womanhood, except for her dark hair. She was large-boned and tall, had piercing blue eyes, and spoke with a sensual huskiness. Hitler had said he liked her, and now I knew why. She was strong, self-possessed, and outgoing.

"I want you to film the Party Rally at Nuremberg this year." I laid my hand on her knee.

She looked down at my hand, then laid hers on top of mine. "Are there conditions?"

"You must always focus on *Der Fürher*. Film others in admiration of him. And, of course, show the enthusiasm of all." I squeezed her knee. "You are as beautiful as Adolf said."

"Beauty fades. I am an artist, *Herr* Goebbels, and that will be my legacy." She pressed on my hand. "These gestures are meaningless." She gently removed my hand from her knee and smiled.

"I do not ask to be in your film, Leni," I said and laid my hand on her heart, "only in your bed occasionally."

She laughed softly.

Actually, I did not ask at all. I simply took her whenever and wherever I wished. She never resisted, but neither did she show interest; she simply participated without any appreciable passion. "Do I not arouse you?" I asked one time.

"The truth is that I am indifferent to you, although sometimes your insistence repels me. There is no compassion in you, Goebbels." She never used my Christian name, as if that would imply a familiarity she didn't want.

I smiled. "I am inflamed with passion for you, Leni, particularly when your cold attitude is contradicted by the heat of your skin, the way your breasts harden, the wetness between your legs. Only your lips lie."

"I cannot control what my body does, responding to the attentions of men and women alike, but my heart and soul belong only to my art."

"I can hold you hostage to your art, Leni. You know I control all of that in Germany. A word from me, and Hitler will know you as nothing more than my whore."

For a moment, her eyes widened with fear. "He respects me," she challenged.

"And how quickly that will change when he sees film of us together. Your crew, Leni," I said, "is easily persuaded to betray you." I leaned back and lit a cigarette. "You already do my bidding. I want final control of your film. It will be called *Der Sieg des Glaubens* – 'The Victory of Faith' – to indicate our victorious takeover of the government because of our faith in Adolf. You are mine, Leni, body and soul."

This rally was the first to be filmed by Leni Riefenstahl, and I immediately recognized her talent. She was unequaled in her ability to present those visual moments and angles which held the greatest meaning and symbolism. She had an innate ability to capture the spontaneous expressions of human enthusiasm as well as to perfectly stage what might imperfectly occur.

During the four days of the Congress, she seemed to be everywhere, directing her crew tirelessly. Each night, she would work from midnight to three, reviewing the rushes and making copious notes in preparation for the following day. Some nights, I took pleasure in making clear to her that the only way she could get back to her film was if she first sexually satisfied me. I told her that I wanted to be bathed in passion, like a purifying fire.

Magda was glad for my dalliance. She was not yet five months pregnant and still yearning herself for a variety of sexual relations. She preferred coupling with the muscled, clumsy Aryan officers in uniform and cleverly presented herself as a timid woman caught by surprise in their embrace.

It was late December 1933 before Riefenstahl's film was completed, and after I'd previewed some of it, I told Leni that we'd give Hitler a premier, private screening. This film demonstrated not just Leni's brilliant filmmaking but my own careful and calculated propaganda in the service of the Party.

Nuremberg was the perfect location and, in fact, it was at this rally that Hitler determined all future rallies would be in Nuremberg. The town was amenable to our cause and the principles of our Party. It was surrounded by a vast, flat field on which we could construct whatever edifices we wished – towers, columns, gleaming white daises – or on which we could gather seemingly endless rows of soldiers, youth, government officials, and seas of huge Nazi flags, their red field, white circle, and black swastika held aloft in Autumn winds. We installed numerous radio and microphone transmitters to amplify speeches, songs, marching music, and the sound of hundreds of thousands of booted marchers.

Leni's images were overwhelming: hundreds of thousands of arms raised in salute, faces serious and enthusiastic, parades filling the streets of Nuremberg. Her visual impact was so immediate and successful that the film needed few title frames to explain the events. And always, as I had bidden, there were shots of Hitler towering over the crowds, or striding confidently among them, or convincing them to agree with him. Leni showed the proud participation of World War One veterans in wheelchairs, on crutches, in uniforms gleaming with medals, the rows of seated officers – generals and admirals buttoned up sharply with their oiled mustaches – and mute, attentive soldiers in perfect rows. And finally, young boys with sweet, fresh faces trying hard to be serious and dedicated but quivering with youthful joy.

When the movie ended, the strip of celluloid flapping loudly in the film reel, and the lights were turned on, Hitler was smiling. "*Danke, danke* – thank you, thank you," he murmured, not wishing to seem too impressed. It was his way to always leave a sliver of doubt about whether or not one's actions had his approval.

"I would like to offer Miss Riefenstahl the position of official cinematographer of the Nazi Party, sir," I said, cupping her elbow in my hand to keep her in full view of Hitler.

He nodded to me and bowed his head to her. "Of course," he said.

"Thank you," Leni answered and gestured as if to curtsy to him.

"I'll see you in bed tonight, dear," I whispered in her ear.

Just before he turned to leave the room, Hitler sighed and said, "Oh, *Fräulein* Riefenstahl, you have complimented me with your photography, but I'm afraid that *Reichleiter* Röhm, with his beer belly and thick neck, will not be so pleased."

I snickered because Röhm, although holding an office equal to mine in the Party, was known to all as a blowhard and a nuisance. We all tolerated him because he had been a former military officer and was a long-time friend of Adolf as well as the founder and leader of the paramilitary *Sturmabteilung,* the SA, which had played a significant part in Hitler's rise to power. Yet, it was true that the years had expanded his waistline with unflattering flab, and his jowls sagged limply.

He was hardly the picture of the perfect Aryan man, and I suspect that Leni had placed him in the film next to Hitler so often as a visually unmistakable contrast to the Führer's trim and handsome figure. I didn't doubt that she had rebuffed his passes.

"Make sure that Hitler has a personal copy of the film. Put the originals and the rushes in the vaults at the Ministry of Propaganda." I leaned in and bit the lobe of Leni's ear until I tasted blood on my teeth.

The Earth Shifts On Its Axis

My second daughter, Hildegarde, was born in 1934. I admit that I was both relieved and disappointed. Still lingering inside of me was a fear that my osteomyelitis was hereditary, yet I yearned for a son who would carry on my name. Despite such ambivalent feelings, I welcomed the beautiful young maiden, my daughter. Magda and I decided that if we were to continue to produce children for the Third Reich — for Hitler — we would bestow on each a name that began with the first letter of the Führer's surname, 'H,' in his honor.

Sometimes, when Magda was asleep or gone to the bed of one of her paramours, I stood in the doorway of my daughters' room and stared at them. Helga was two, Hildegarde not yet one, and their innocence touched me. Were they to one day discover that they'd lived past lives? I could not imagine, given their sweet, smooth faces, clear, blue eyes, and curly blonde hair, that they were not the first and most unblemished of whatever successive lives they would live on earth. They had inherited their looks from their mother, who had not, under hypnosis, discovered previous lives of her own, so perhaps they were blessed in the same way, free of night terrors.

As for me, I accepted what others would have deemed shortcomings or weaknesses in my previous lives: a priest who was not only sexually promiscuous but perverted as well, a friar whose twisted religious devotion led him to extreme masochism. I simply accepted these behaviors, seeing no need to correct them or seek forgiveness for them. On the contrary, I derived pleasure from them and intended to intensify the behaviors, thereby increasing my own satisfaction. I always carried the coin Magda gave me and I clutched it in my pocket now. Was I being a true disciple, I thought, of Dionysius?

The affair with Leni had cooled; she remained in my stable of women that I could call upon any time I wished, but my physical attraction to her had fallen to the level of ordinary. When there was nothing new to discover about a woman or when she could not arouse me in any surprising way, it was over between us.

Besides, I had made Magda pregnant during one of our obligatory couplings (she assured me that I was the prospective father since she was careful with other lovers), and here in mid-June, she was three months along. Magda decided, without any basis in science at all, that if she remained faithful to our marriage during this pregnancy, we would surely have a boy. I chided her for such foolishness, but I did not object to her staying at home and becoming a *hausfrau*. She requested that I practice celibacy during this time as well. I made fun of the idea but agreed to Magda's wish nonetheless. Still, I would be surprised if we'd produced a boy.

In addition, I was watching a drama unfold within the ranks of our cabinet, Hitler's group of *Reichleiters*. We had always been a fractious group, brought together solely by our devotion to Adolf. We did not always agree with his political goals, but we had seen, time after time, that if what he wanted was carried out to the letter, success followed. We had won political credulity, toppled the old Weimar government, and captured the hearts of the German people. Now, we only needed to maintain peace and ensure prosperity.

"All of you paid lip service to his ideas, but I acted on them," Röhm said at a cabinet meeting. Hitler was absent that day, vacationing with his mistress, Eva, in the Bavarian Alps.

"Shut up, Ernst," Göring complained. "You are always stirring a pot about something."

"And eating greedily from it," Himmler said sarcastically, referring to Röhm's bulging waistline.

Everyone laughed. Röhm's face reddened with anger. "It was I who created the SA to fight Adolf's battles in the early days. It was I who nurtured a military force of volunteers to enforce Adolf's wishes. It was I who, by last year, raised an army of three million. And now we can stage a wonderful coup to decisively bring Germany under our control."

"But it is you," I reminded him, "who refuses to control your army, a force made up largely of malcontents and thugs.

Don't you think the Führer would disapprove?"

"He can be short-sighted sometimes. But you, Goebbels," he said, pointing to me, "have only words." He grunted. "And, of course, your reputation as a rutting ram." He paused. Then, "Our revolution is not yet over. We must continue forward, throw the old bureaucrats out the windows, make a clean sweep with the force of my broom, the Storm Troopers." He remained standing, hoping to hear murmurs of agreement from us. When none came, he sat down heavily. "You are making a mistake, gentleman. The revolution is still brewing."

Long after the meeting was over, Himmler called me at home. "So, what do you think?"

"Of what?" I was wracking my brain trying to think of a theme for this year's Party Congress in early September.

"Of crazy Röhm, of course."

"Oh, just that. Crazy. He has raised an army and wants to give them something to do, that's all," I said.

"So, you think he is just a blowhard."

"Yes, of course. Hasn't he always been so? Sometimes, I think he just needs a woman to drive him crazy and keep him in bed." I thought of the young actress – what was her name? – I had bedded the other night. Perhaps I should send her to Röhm with a note: "From the rutting ram."

"I think he is dangerous," Himmler said without humor. "He implies that Hitler is only a step towards something greater, not the true savior of Germany. Besides, he would not be convinced if you sent him one of your actress women, Joseph. I hear he salivates only after some of the young members of his Storm Troopers."

"Heinrich," I responded, "his degeneracy, distasteful as it is, hurts no one. But your remarks about Röhm's ambitions are accusations of treason, which you suggest, I think because you cannot hide your desire to take over his SA." I laughed. Then, I cautioned, "You know that he is close to Adolf."

"You're blind if you don't see Röhm's ambition, Joseph. Don't lie now."

"It is my job to lie, Heinrich. But in this, I tell the truth: Adolf likes Röhm." I refused to be drawn into Himmler's plot to backstab Röhm, which I knew was the purpose of this phone call. "What does Göring say?"

"He, too, is alarmed by Röhm's remarks. It is Göring who suggested I call you."

So, I thought it was not just Himmler. Those of us in the inner circle wanted, first and foremost, to be favored by Adolf. Sometimes, this was accomplished by deeds which we knew would please the Fürher. Other times, it could be achieved by plotting against each other, and this was best succeeded with accomplices. However, our collaborations were temporary at best and, we all knew, for a singular purpose. Once the goal was achieved, we retreated to our respective corners to distrusting one another. "What are you planning?" I asked calmly.

"Will you oppose us?" Himmler asked cautiously.

"You know me, Heinrich. I detest violence, but I will not stop it. If I benefit, or if I am left untouched, I will not stand in anyone's way. I am neutral in all things except my fidelity to Hitler and the Third Reich." He didn't have to believe me; he just had to hear me say these words to assuage his misgivings.

"Göring wants to know if you will visit Hitler and speak to him." There was a pause. Then Himmler said sarcastically, "Because you are neutral."

"Actually, I have a reason to see Adolf. There is a fellow I hope will be given a government position."

"In Propaganda? Don't you have enough staff to choke on, Joseph?" Himmler said.

"No, I have my fill. This fellow, Albert Speer, is a brilliant architect. He will enhance our image worldwide with his ideas for monuments."

"So, you will go see Adolph while he's with Eva in the

Alps? Best bring along Magda to make it a family vacation. Please tell him about Ernst's ambitions."

"We'll see how the conversation goes. I make no promises, Heinrich." I'd already made up my mind that Röhm's ambitions, although dangerous, were none of my business. Hitler did not like to be told that he was being deceived; I would not incur his wrath by being the one to betray Röhm to him.

Hitler had recently purchased Berghof after having vacationed there a few times. It was a cozy cottage tucked into the Alps. Adolph had recently gotten involved with a girl twenty years younger, Eva Braun, although he insisted to us that it was not a serious relationship.

Hitler had confessed to Magda and me when he was sometimes feeling sad that his great love was Geli Raubal, his half-niece, nineteen years his junior. She moved into Hitler's Munich apartment when she began her medical studies at University, and soon after, much to his disapproval, started an affair with his chauffeur. For the next six years, he kept a tight leash on her, never allowing her to go out anywhere alone. Eventually, she declared her desire to study singing in Vienna, but she and Hitler argued because he refused to let her go. When he went to a meeting in Nuremberg, Geli used his pistol to kill herself. She was just twenty-three.

Although Hitler had met Eva Braun before Geli's suicide, it was only afterward that he began a relationship with her, unfazed by the fact that he was twenty-three years older than her. Much less sophisticated and educated than many of our wives and mistresses, Eva seemed to us to be more suited to being Hitler's casual mistress; she would not, we thought, survive in the rarefied atmosphere of competition among the official Nazi wives.

Magda and I arrived in the early evening when twilight sparkled on the mountain snow. Hitler greeted us cheerfully, especially Magda, who, I knew, he sincerely liked. "Here they are," he said, hugging us both, "the First Family of the Third Reich."

"The children are still in Berlin, Adolf. I thought it best." This was my signal to him that this was not merely a friendly visit. "I hope you understand, *mein Führer*." The look in his eye indicated that he understood when I switched from the familiar 'Adolph' to his formal title.

He nodded. "Perhaps after dinner, Magda can entertain Eva with stories of her childhood while we talk, Joseph."

"Of course."

Nightfall in the Alps was like nowhere else, for the icy coldness seemed to wrap its unseen arms around me, dampening any hot passions stirring within. Adolf and I sat by the fire smoking fat Villiger cigars.

"I am still amazed with Leni Reifenstahl's talent, Joseph. I look forward to more of her movies."

"Yes, I agree."

Hitler chuckled. "You know, Ernst was embarrassed when I chided him about how fat he looked in that film. But he is a great ally nonetheless." Hitler watched the smoke rise from his cigar.

"He is close to you, eh, *mein Führer*?" I asked.

"What? Of course." Hitler snapped out of his reverie, immediately aware of my change of tone.

"Röhm advocates for change." I chose my words carefully.

"Ernst is impatient, that is all. He knows that I want to proceed cautiously, to curry the favor of business and industry as well as of the people; otherwise, our plans for complete control, indeed for expansion, will not be realized."

"He complains that all of us in your cabinet are worthless fools."

"And so you would be if you gave his complaints purchase. Besides, whose opinion do all of you most trust, Röhm's or mine?" Adolf smiled, but his tone was challenging.

"Of course, yours," I answered immediately, leaning forward and smiling broadly.

"Then understand that Ernst Röhm is a close friend of mine and, unless I am otherwise convinced, he will be considered a valuable member of our Party."

"I understand," I said. "I am sorry, *mein Führer*, to have misunderstood Röhm's friendship with you." There. I could tell Himmler I'd talked to Adolf but could not change his mind about Röhm. It was only half a lie.

"On another matter, I am recommending an architect to you, Albert Speer. Please hear out his ideas for the Third Reich."

"Thank you," Himmler said in a phone call to me mere days after my visit with Hitler in the Alps. "I will approach *der Führer* myself now; he is bound to accept our revelation. Göring and I will put everything in motion so that Hitler cannot help but act against Röhm. A clean sweep and your cooperation will not be forgotten, Joseph."

I didn't have to wait long to see what he meant. I was pressed into service afterward for what was codenamed *Kolibri* (Hummingbird). Behind the scenes, Göring transferred control of his political police (his Gestapo) to Himmler, who had already transformed his SS (the *Shutzstaffel*) into an elite corps loyal only to himself and Hitler. The two then developed a list of those to be executed, topped by Röhm, who they portrayed as the most dangerous enemy of the Nazi Party.

On June 30th, Hitler summoned me and Himmler to fly with him to Munich. "What's going on?" Magda asked me as I hurried out the door.

"I think it's *Der Röhm Putsch* – the Röhm Coup," I told her; Himmler and Göring had given the plot this name between themselves.

"Be careful."

We flew to Munich and drove in an entourage of black

sedans at top speed to the headquarters of the local SA leader, who was also chief of police.

"You failed to keep the peace last night," Hitler complained to the man standing at attention before him. He was referring to a rampage in the streets of Munich conducted by the SA the night before.

"We were, perhaps, overenthusiastic in our desire to put down the protest," the man, a leader of the local SA, said, smiling. "We acted in accordance with General Röhm's intentions."

Hitler became enraged. "You think yourself clever?" he asked. Suddenly, he reached out and tore the epaulets from the man's shirt. "You were supposed to maintain the peace! You have betrayed me!" Hitler turned to his guards, *"Verhafte ihn! – Take him."* He wiped the spittle from his mustache.

"Röhm and his officers are in Bad Wiessee," Himmler announced. "We can be there within the hour."

Hitler nodded and frowned.

The ride to Bad Wiessee was tense. Hitler was silent, pressed into a corner of the back seat, his arms folded across his chest. None of us spoke. Himmler started to hum under his breath but stopped when Hitler shot him an angry glance.

We arrived before seven a.m., the sun rising slowly from the horizon. Himmler's SS stormed the hotel, waking all of the Storm Troopers' leadership, including Röhm. Two of the SA officers, one of them just eighteen, were found in bed together. Hitler, further enraged, ordered their immediate execution; a few moments later, I heard the two shots in the courtyard outside. Röhm and the others were bundled into sedans to be taken back to Munich.

"Danke, Heinrich. You have done a great service to Germany," Hitler said to Himmler as we sped back to Munich, where Himmler had arranged an assemblage for Hitler to address. He turned to me and sighed. "You see how depravity and perversity must be dealt with, my dear Joseph? Follow suit and burn all copies of Riefenstahl's film in which I am seen too often

with that scum, Röhm. He has been a deep disappointment to me."

I nodded, already planning a broadcast upon my return to Berlin denouncing "the moral turpitude of traitors to Germany." I suggested quietly, "Shall we retain a single copy of *The Victory of Faith* for your personal library, Sir?"

He nodded. In Munich, Hitler eagerly addressed the crowd, vowing that all such disobedience would be annihilated. He described Röhm as one who had acted contrary to Hitler's wishes that the National Socialist revolution turn itself into an evolutionary force; Röhm was, therefore, the worst traitor in world history. Of course, the crowd roared its agreement and approval, even though the difference between revolution – carnage in the streets – and evolution – biding one's time and currying favor – escaped them. It was Hitler's sincerity and confident manner that convinced them.

All of us slept, if fitfully, during the four-hour plane trip back to Berlin. When we emerged from the plane, unkempt and unshaven, we mumbled farewells to one another and headed off in different directions.

It was ten a.m. when I arrived home. Magda and the girls were not there, the girls having gone to school, and Magda having gone only God knows where. I called Göring. "*Kolibri*" is all I said as instructed by Himmler; later, I found out it would begin the killings of all enemies, old and new, that would last for two more days. I went to bed.

By the end of the purge, three days later, on July 2nd, I still did not have accurate numbers of those who were killed, only having reports of eighty-five ranking officials executed. I was sure that, if I considered the arrests of low-level SA members, the number would be more. However, not wanting to alarm the German people, I prevented the newspapers from publishing lists of the dead, and Göring commanded the destruction of all police records for the three days of the action. On July 2nd, I addressed the nation by radio, explaining that Hitler had narrowly prevented Röhm from overthrowing the government and sending Germany into turmoil.

A week later, I was in bed with Leni Riefenstahl when she asked, "Where is that ugly toad Röhm now?"

"Himmler tells me, with glee, that he is dead," I answered. I laid my head on Leni's breasts and rested my hand on her warm thigh. "Two of Himmler's men visited him in Stadelheim Prison a few days ago, handed him a pistol loaded with a single cartridge, and told him he had ten minutes to kill himself."

"So he died honorably," Leni said.

"Hardly," I said. "He told them that if he was to be killed, it should be at Adolf's hand alone. They left, waited ten minutes, and returned to find him bare-chested and defiant."

"So they shot him," Leni concluded. "You Nazis are so boring. You should have at least tortured him until he begged for death; it would have made a wonderfully dramatic story."

"I do not like the nickname 'Nazis.' We are the National Socialists, and we want only justice," I argued.

"You want blood," she insisted. "You have betrayed those who most supported you at the beginning, the revolutionaries who wanted to change Germany."

"We have matured. We understand that change comes through evolution now," I explained.

"So you murder the revolutionaries!" She shook her head. "Poor dumb Röhm."

"Perhaps you are right, Leni. You know, Hitler had me burn all but one copy of your film."

"My film! But why?"

"Too many shots of Röhm with Adolf. It would suggest he was duped by the man."

She was angry to have been drawn into the drama. "Perhaps he was," she said petulantly.

"Hitler has the sole copy now. You haven't kept a copy yourself, have you?"

She brushed aside my question. "My film of this year's Party Congress will be far better. What do you think of the title *Triumph of the Will*?"

"Quite appropriate. But this time, Leni. . . ."

"Yes, yes. Hitler will be the exclusive star," she agreed. "The *Führer* himself has told me that I am to produce the film with only his approvals."

"You mean not me?" I asked, alarmed that I was being excluded.

"So it seems, Joseph. Well, we had better enjoy ourselves now," and she started to kiss me before I could ask again if she kept a copy of that earlier film.

Less than two weeks later, Hitler agreed to address the Reichstag about the Röhm affair. I helped him craft his speech in which he said, "I was responsible for the fate of the German people, and thereby, I became the supreme judge of the German people. I gave the order to shoot the ringleaders. . . .If anyone raises his hand to strike the State, then certain death is his fate." The members of the Reichstag gave him a standing ovation and shouts of *Heil Hitler! Heil Führer!*

As Hitler stood on the dais grinning proudly, someone began the old 1928 song "*Wetzt die langen Messer* – Sharpen the Long Knives", which the Party had popularized to encourage antisemitism. I thought it just as appropriate to this event whereby we had unequivocally established Hitler as our leader with unconstrained power, and beyond the reach of traditional law and order.

Respite

I realized that I had spent nearly every waking hour of the last twelve years of my life in the service of the Nazi Party and *mein Führer*, Adolf Hitler. I yearned to turn my attention to my own interests and concerns while boosting my own reputation with Adolf.

The so-called Night of the Long Knives, although not orchestrated by me, was accepted by the German public because of my propaganda efforts. It was, in fact, a suspension of the rule of law insofar as the elected government, in the body of Adolf Hitler, suspended all the trappings of democratic government in order to accomplish swift judgment on those who could be seen as dangerous to our government. We didn't bother with courts and trials; we simply exterminated those who conspired against us.

Or, at least, those who could be *construed* to have conspired against us. I knew that Hitler's rage against Röhm was the result of evidence provided by Himmler and Göring, and they had been encouraged by the leaders of the German army who feared the possibility that Röhm's paramilitary group would eventually absorb them. How much of that evidence was true, I did not question. If Adolf believed it, so did I. And it was my responsibility to ensure that the public also believed it. I did a good job: in August 1934, we ministers of the cabinet passed the "Law on the Allegiance of Civil Servants and Soldiers of the Armed Forces", which required swearing an oath of loyalty to Hitler personally rather than to the State. I was proud of my work but tired of the constant need not only to defend our policies but also to personally curry the Führer's favor.

"Are you complaining?" Magda asked me as she put a robe on over her negligee. She rang a small bell on her night table to summon the nanny to the children's rooms.

"No, no," I answered impatiently. "Why are you sending Lizbeth to the children's rooms?" She was distracting me from attaching the leather straps of the brace to my leg.

"It's seven a.m.; they will be waking up. I don't want them running into our room this morning." She sat on the edge of the bed and lit a cigarette. "I want to tell you what I dreamed last night."

"Was it about me?" I laughed. Instead of putting on my trousers, I sat down on my side of the bed, then hoisted my braced leg onto the rumpled duvet and sat with my back against the bed's headboard.

Magda handed me her cigarette while she rearranged herself to lay back on the bed, her head in my lap. "About you, yes, but also about me." She caressed the inside of my thigh. "Should we have more children?"

"We have five, Magda. I think that is enough, especially since we have been lucky with a son only once. And this year, we had Hedwig." I took a puff of her cigarette and handed it back to her. "Tell me about your dream."

"I think Adolf would like us to have more children," Magda mused. "We are the exemplar German family to him." She squeezed my thigh. "And we have not made love for quite some time."

I pushed her hand aside. "I have been exhausted, Magda, with party politics. Besides, the best way to avoid another child – despite Adolf's desires – is to avoid sex. I'm afraid I am too virile."

Magda laughed scornfully and sat up. "You think I haven't known all along about Lidá Baarová, your Czech whore? Only Adolf is ignorant of your affair with her, and I could make sure that he, too, will soon know."

I snorted. "And will you also tell him about your carrying on with Hanke?" I had only discovered a week before that my secretary, Karl Hanke, was involved with Magda. "How long has that been going on?"

"Your affair with Lidá has been the talk of Berlin for two years. Did you expect me to just sit at home and wait for your return? Karl has been sympathetic for a month now."

"So that's what you call your fucking – 'sympathy'?" I sneered at her. "Let us just say we understand one another. And no more talk of empty retaliation when we are both guilty of the same thing. Now," I sighed, "what of your dream?"

"It was nothing, Joseph. We were in bed together with Adolf." She shrugged, no longer amused by her dream or wanting to share it with me.

"Was he between us?" I asked absently.

"Yes." She stood up again, headed for the children's rooms.

"As he always is," I remarked. "I hope we were both enjoying making love to him. He seems to be our fatal attraction, eh?" Instead of displaying my annoyance with Magda, I simply swung my legs out of bed onto the floor. "I'll be home late. Shall we take the children to the zoo this weekend?"

"We'll see," Magda answered as she left the room.

The work at the ministry had almost settled into a routine. After ten years of public opinion being reshaped through a carefully designed and executed program of propaganda, I felt I had finally united Germany in its devotion to Hitler. Our party controlled all media, decided the content and direction of educational institutions, and infiltrated family structures by indoctrinating German youth into paramilitary organizations such as *Bund Deutscher Mädel* – League of German Girls – and *Hitlerjugend* – Hitler Youth.

There were a few protests but little resistance, thanks in part to Himmler's immediate response to any opposition by imprisonment in Dachau but also because I kept a watchful eye on public communication in Germany. My current worry was a Lutheran pastor named Niemöller, who had suddenly decided to question our handling of the "Jewish problem."

Niemöller had, in fact, been an early supporter of National Socialism and the rise of Adolf Hitler. Like us, he believed in a national revival of Germany to its former state of power on the European stage. Yet, as much as he expressed a clear anti-

Semitism similar to our own, he began to vocally distinguish those Jews who had converted to Christianity and those Christians who had Jews in their background. To him, they were Christians and, therefore, to be protected from any discrimination by the government. That belief led Niemöller, with other clergy like Karl Barth and Dietrich Bonhoeffer, to found what they called the "Confessing Church." This was a movement arising from the formation of the German Evangelical Church, a confederation of Protestant churches sympathetic to our policies and politics.

I thought these religious disputes were beneath me. Hitler had handled the minority German Catholics by promising the pope some autonomy in Germany; of course, it was a lie, but the lie in service of a greater good is acceptable. He expected me to deal with the German Protestants similarly. Seeing that Niemöller was only interested in maintaining a semblance of church sovereignty, I allowed him a great deal of latitude, knowing that so far, he had no political quarrel with Hitler. Unless a threat to our control was overt, we were smarter to treat our internal enemies as nothing more than recalcitrant children.

So, with spies everywhere, I felt I could indulge my private life more frequently. And that is how I became involved with Lidá Baarová. She and her then-fiancé, the German actor Gustav Frölich, moved in next door to me at one of my residences just outside of Berlin. Because my office was the sole arbiter of what films could be made and shown in Germany, I already knew Frölich. Baarová, twelve years his junior, immediately struck me as the Czech equivalent of Marlene Dietrich, who had refused our offer to become the "beautiful face" of the Third Reich.

"I hope you will stay in Berlin and continue to make films here," I'd said to her at our first meeting in 1936 when she was just twenty. "You remind me of Marlene Dietrich," I said.

"I think you are trying to seduce me, Reichminister," she answered, blushing.

She had what I would describe as "smoky eyes" that

looked at me without modesty or timidity. Her eyes promised passion. And her eyebrows were shaped like thin dark wings of seduction. "It would only be fair, for you have already conquered me," I responded. And so our affair began, for I could not resist her natural charms. I had, of course, bedded all the beautiful women in the German film industry, whether stars or ingenues, directors, or script girls. But Lidá was different. When Hitler met her, I could see that he, too, was immediately taken with her beauty. He complimented her by saying that he had a photograph of her on his bedside table. I knew that was not true, for he kept, instead, a photo of his half-niece Geli Raubal. However, his remark made me realize that Lidá bore a resemblance to Geli, and it made me wonder if Adolf and I had similar tastes in women.

At first, Magda did not care. After all, even though I was seeing Lidá every night, I managed to get Magda pregnant six months into my assignation with Lidá. Thus, I kept Magda preoccupied, if not completely satisfied. Moreover, I was infatuated with Lidá because, despite my being fourteen years older, she insisted that I was satisfying her completely. Her fiancé, Frölich, rapidly released her from their engagement.

After a few months of seeing her privately, I decided that to be seen with her publicly was not outrageous. After all, most of my colleagues in the party had both wives and mistresses and with our control of all public media, there was no danger of a scandal. Nevertheless, I kept a private suite at the Kaiserhof, the grand hotel in the municipal section of Berlin, and it was there that Lidá and I retired one night.

"What do you see in me?" I asked her as we lay in bed.

"You mean, aside from the sex?" she asked coquettishly.

"Or, including," I offered.

"I was told your nickname is 'the ram.' Your power is intoxicating. You seem to control everything, and that excites me, body and soul. I cannot refuse you."

I wondered if that was why I was so besotted with her — because she so admired me. It was a strange feeling. "And how do you feel about my twisted leg?" I asked, throwing the cover off us, exposing my shriveled limb. The brace lay on the floor on my side of the bed.

"I don't think about it, Joseph. It is inconsequential."

"What if I told you to kiss it now, Lidá? To caress it? To admire it?" I liked to dare women to defy me.

She was lying in bed to my left. Without looking at my leg, she said, "Why?"

"To prove your love. You said you admire my control. Can I control you, Lidá?" I rolled over on my side to face her. My crippled leg flopped closer to her. "Go ahead. Touch it, Kiss it."

She looked into my eyes. "You should take my word for it, Joseph. But I will do as you ask." She reached for the leg.

"You know," I said later, turning onto my back again, "your surrender to me is like a drug. I don't care that my wife says she will ask Hitler for permission to divorce me. What do you think?"

"I don't think she will do it. But if she does, I think it will hurt you, Joseph, and I think you will blame me."

"I don't think she will do it either. Come, let's not talk anymore. Come closer, *meine Liebste* – my dearest love."

Lidá was offered a contract by the American studio Metro-Goldwyn-Mayer in 1937, and although she teased me with the idea of leaving for the States, she eventually declined their offer, explaining that she was in love with me.

I began to think that I would be happier divorced from Magda and as one of Adolf's ambassadors with Lidá at my side; it was my daydream. Hitler ordered me across the square to his offices. After almost no small talk, he said, "I did not think you so stupid, Joseph," he began.

"Sir?" I sat up, alert to some trouble coming.

"This Czech actress you are seeing, Lidá Baarová." He

leaned forward in the heavily-stuffed chair.

"What do you mean?" I straightened my shoulders.

"She came to see me, Joseph. She worries about you as if she were your wife," Adolf said and frowned. He pushed a lock of hair off his forehead.

"She's a foolish girl, Sir. Nothing more." I smiled sweetly.

"Do you love her? Like Magda?" Adolf stood up and straightened his jacket. He looked down at me, putting his hands on his hips.

"Of course not," I insisted. I was angry that Lidá had apparently dared to approach Hitler, and I was disappointed that this would signal the end of us because I had lost face with Hitler.

"Then you must give her up immediately. You have the perfect marriage that sets the example for all of the Third Reich. You cannot destroy that." He turned and strode to the window.

"Magda and I have an understanding, Sir." I hoped to convince Adolf that my affair was not a significant matter.

"Do you understand that this woman is not Aryan? She is a Czech. She is beneath us." Adolf insisted. His back was to me, but the tone of his voice was clearly full of warning.

"She is not Aryan, but she is no Jew," I argued.

He turned to face me. "Have you not been listening, Joseph? It is time for Germany to live again as the power it was meant to be! One of my plans is to annex Sudetenland, to bring the Germans living there back into the loving bosom of Germany." I could see a mist of spittle coming from his mouth as he spoke.

Adolf was referring to some of the lands inhabited by German speakers but owned in the ninth century by Bohemia and integrated after World War I into the new country of Czechoslovakia. His intention was to annex those lands – in the northern, southern, and western parts of Czechoslovakia – to Nazi Germany. "But what has that to do with Lidá?" I asked.

"*Dumkopf!*" he shouted, losing his temper. "I will not have one of my Reichministers held in sway by a woman, by a Czech woman!" He stared angrily at me.

I was paralyzed by his outburst, never having been the target of his wrath. I simply nodded.

"Or, you could resign your position with the party. I'm sure there is someone who will be more obedient to my wishes." Adolf turned back to the window and peered out, his back stiff. It was his way of reproaching me.

"I will do as you ask, Sir. Please, just give me some time." Losing my position with Hitler suddenly seemed more important than anything else. So, I intended to move Lidá out of Berlin and out of the public eye, but I could not give up the woman who adored me. Nor could I surrender my place in the Party which I had worked so hard to secure.

I learned later, after Lidá disappeared from our hotel suite with all her belongings, that she was visited by Berlin's Chief of Police, who told her that, on Hitler's orders, she was forbidden from performing in films in Germany and that she would be followed day and night to make sure she did not contact me. Her latest film was banned before its premiere.

I learned through sources that eventually, Lidá had a nervous breakdown and found herself, again on Hitler's orders, prevented from leaving the country. At the end of the year, with assistance from a few friends, she fled to Prague. I dared not write her or otherwise contact her.

Then I thought of my previous lives and how those two men had taken control of their lives and done what best suited them, what most pleased them. I felt belittled by the thought of their defiance and their courage in pursuing their goals, even to death. I began to think that there had to be some idea that I could devote my life to while currying greater favor with Hitler. Since the Baarová affair, he had grown distant from me, and I knew he was watching for weakness in me.

In my previous lives, I had been successful in my goals, unfettered by an attachment to a woman. Was that the key to my success? I shrugged. I could not, like them, be celibate. Perhaps enjoying the company of women was my particular weakness.

I went back to Magda contritely, explaining to her that I had been momentarily infatuated but was now recommitting myself to our marriage and our shared goal of serving the Third Reich. To that end, I proposed that we start work on having another child. Magda put aside her affair with Karl Hanke; I made it easy for her to do so when I transferred him to a post in Munich. I revealed to Magda what Hitler had said to me.

"How are we to return to his good graces?" Magda asked, worried. She enjoyed her position as Germany's "First Wife," and she was not happy about having to surrender it to gossip.

"Now that all of Germany is under his control, now that he feels secure nationally, he is beginning to eye territory beyond our borders, like he did with Sudetenland. But if he turns his attention there, I will be pushed further into the background. My Ministry of Propaganda thrives on national issues. There must be something at home, so to speak, with which we can regain Adolf's attention."

"Then you must convince him that there is a tangible threat within Germany which he must attend to and for which you can provide a solution. Think, Joseph."

I slapped my knee. "I think I have it, Magda. I will enlist the help of Himmler in this because his resources are best suited to the task, but I will set in motion an event that Adolf cannot ignore and which, if it works out as I plan, he will always see as my crowning demonstration of loyalty and devotion."

"What are you planning?"

"Let me work out the details before I tell you, Magda, but I already see it as the natural progression from the hugely successful book burnings. Brilliant, Magda, it will be brilliant. You'll see."

It's Not the Same Old Song

The song we sung when Hitler purged the party of disloyal traitors, the old 1928 song "*Wetzt die langen Messer – Sharpen the Long Knives*", was so popular that its title replaced what we first called "Röhm's Putsch"; once it was reported worldwide, the event became known as "The Night of the Long Knives." It was a misnomer insofar as the assassinations and imprisonments took place over more than a single night, but no matter, the Nazi Party became known for its strength and decisiveness in dealing with its enemies. Its opening lyric was:

Wetzt die langen Messer   Sharpen the long knives.

Laßt die Messer flutschen   On the sidewalk!

auf dem Bürgersteig!   Let the knives slide

in den Judenleib!   Into the Jewish body !

My antipathy towards Communists was part and parcel of my support for the Fascists who, like me, believed in the necessity for a strong and independent Germany. On the other hand, Hitler's avowed antisemitism was less obvious in me, though at his suggestion, I gladly assisted in legislation and even extralegal activities that were clearly antisemitic in intent. For my own protection, I had to continually downplay my prior associations with Jews: professors who'd mentored me in my studies, girlfriends who I'd romanced, and colleagues at newspapers and journals. To me, Jews were essentially a political threat who espoused communism. So, whenever provided with the opportunity to show that I stood with my Aryan brothers in anti-Jewish sentiment, I participated with enthusiasm; it took me a bit longer to see the Jews as more than a political threat and to view them as a serious racial threat to our Aryanism.

I had already, as commanded by Adolf, taken some steps against both gypsies and Jews, but especially the Jews since

Hitler expressed the most animosity towards them. I, myself, did not share the depth of that animosity, largely because I did not understand its rationale. I had in my life, prior to the rise of the Nazi Party, dealings with Jews that were both congenial and positive. I was privileged to study at university with some Jewish professors; in fact, I earned my doctorate under the mentorship of Max Freiherr von Waldberg, a Jew.

Moreover, I never forgot my affair with that half-Jewish girl, Else Janke, a school teacher in my hometown. It was easy to fall in love with this woman who adored me, especially because she served to lift me from my depression over breaking up with Anka Stalherm. Yet, I knew it was a doomed relationship that could not overcome her unfortunate background. I could not blame her for what she had no control over, but I also could not ignore my responsibility to be true to my own race.

Exiled to the periphery of Hitler's inner circle since my romance with Lidá Baarová, I was desperate to return to the Führer's good graces, and I decided that I could most easily accomplish this by turning his attention to what I termed "the enemy within," the non-Aryan population that lived within the borders of our beloved Germany. That is, the gypsies and the Jews.

So, when Hitler spoke to us, his cabinet, yet again about his disgust with the number of Jews still in Germany, I searched for ways to institute further restrictions on them. Instead, fate provided me with the perfect propaganda.

On November 7th, 1938, a minor German official stationed in our Paris embassy, Ernst vom Rath, was assassinated by a young teenaged Polish Jew. The young man's parents, Polish Jews living in Germany for eight years, had recently been expelled with thousands of others; denied entry back to Poland, they were basically stranded without a country. Their young son, failing to make a successful appeal on their behalf, shot vom Rath.

Two days later, on the anniversary of the first Nazi putsch in 1923, I made the assassination the mainstay of my purposefully-inflammatory speech to the Party, suggesting that it was "World Jewry" that conspired to effect the killing in retaliation for Germany's new laws to control them. And, in the same breath, I explained that Hitler wanted no organized retaliation, although spontaneous responses would not be hampered. Then, I sat back and waited.

Party leaders throughout Germany had heard my radio address; spontaneous violence began to erupt later that evening and just after midnight. Reinhard Heydrich, the chief of Security Police, consulted with the cabinet and sent urgent cables to all State police and SA leaders with specific directives: do not interfere with actions taken by the SA or Hitler Youth units, but insure that they refrain from damaging non-Jewish property; do not attack foreigners or Germans; remove and transfer to security forces all significant material from synagogues and related Jewish properties; finally, because they were "the cause of the unrest," arrest as many Jews as local jails could hold, especially young, healthy men.

More than 900 synagogues were destroyed, burning throughout the night. Firefighters were told to intervene only if nearby structures were threatened. More than seven thousand Jewish commercial establishments were looted and their windows shattered. Jewish cemeteries were desecrated. The event came to be known as *Kristallnacht* – The Night of Broken Glass – for the shattered glass littering the streets that night. Almost a hundred Jews were killed.

Most significantly, around thirty thousand Jewish males were arrested and sent to concentration camps. Jews throughout Germany, Austria, and those areas we had reclaimed from Czechoslovakia began to entertain thoughts of emigration. To underline our serious attitude regarding Jews, we enacted new, strict policies: Jewish businesses could only reopen if managed by non-Jews, Jewish children were forbidden from attending school, and Jews were barred from selling goods and services, from managerial positions, and from practicing any crafts. Our investigations into *Kristallnacht* resulted in the government imposing a one-billion mark fine on the Jewish community for the destruction we found *they* had caused that night.

I was in my office, staring out at the plaza, pleased with what I had caused to happen and thinking about how Hitler would wholeheartedly take me back into his good graces as a result of this devastation. As much as I hated the Jews, I admitted that their word, derived from Russian, for what we had accomplished appeared more descriptive, less negative: *pogrom*.

My secretary opened the door hesitantly.

"Yes, Fraulein Pomsel, what is it?" I asked, turning from the window.

"Here are the reports on those arrested in *Kristallnacht*." She placed the pages on my desk.

"*Danke.* Is there something else?" I noted that she had not moved to leave.

"If I may ask, Herr Reich Minister Doktor Goebbels."

"Yes?" I was amused but also pleased that she had used *all* of my titles in addressing me.

"There are rumors in the street that all the Jews are going to Dachau and such for harsh punishment." She looked upset.

"Those who broke the law, of course, yes. For those, however, who have lost their homes and livelihoods, our government takes pity on them. We are relocating them to villages in Sudetenland (the area on the Czech border with Germany) that need repopulating. There they will find ample land and friendly neighbors who will welcome their arrival with open arms." The lie came easily; why confirm the rumors or her suspicion?

Brunhilde Pomsel sighed and smiled. "I told my neighbors that we shouldn't worry. The National Socialists have Germany's well-being in mind. We won't be disappointed."

"Yes," I nodded enthusiastically, "tell your friends that *der Führer* loves his people and would do nothing to harm them."

When she departed, I thought how effective the combination of ignorance and awe could be in the hands of a master propagandist as myself. The thought sexually aroused me, and I thought again how much I missed Lidá Baarová. I shrugged. No matter. When I went home tonight, Magda would be there, and she would suffice to satisfy me and keep the nightmares at bay.

Kristallnacht did, indeed, bring me back into Hitler's circle of intimates, although my position remained somewhat precarious because others were jockeying so desperately to be his favorite among us. With the annexation of the Sudetenland, the Czech regions, Hitler's appetite for German expansion was whetted, and he was more interested in the geopolitics of Europe than in the internal policies of German life. In such a climate, I was not excluded, but I was sidelined except when I could bring the cabinet discussions around to how our dominance over Europe had to include the continued expulsion of the Jews from all societies, German and otherwise.

"*Lebensraum*," Hitler said angrily, pounding the table with his fist, "we need room to live and thrive as Germans."

Everyone was silent, so I cleared my throat and spoke. "For those of you who don't know, the term was coined by Friedrich Ratzel, a geographer and ethnographer who applied Darwin's theory of survival of the fittest to nations."

"So, we must acquire territory and resources to survive," Göring commented.

"It is no different from the Americans' idea of 'manifest destiny,' gentlemen," Hitler lectured. "Their treatment of the Indians, like ours of the Slavs and Jews, is based on the superiority and the privilege of the white race."

"And only the fittest and most powerful of nations will prevail," I added.

"That is us," Hitler said. "But to achieve our destiny of world domination, we must acquire – by force, if necessary – territory. And what territories, gentlemen, would most enrich us?"

We all knew the answer, for Hitler had told us many times. East of Germany – especially Russian lands – were the natural resources and agricultural riches that would enhance us. "But we have agreements to consider," Joachim von Ribbentrop, the Reichminister of Foreign Affairs, protested. He had been instrumental in recently completing a non-aggression pact with Stalin in Soviet Russia. Its terms not only included a guaranteed 10-year peace between Russia and Germany but also a definition of the spheres of influence each country would exert across the Slavic countries of Poland, Lithuania, Latvia, Estonia, and Finland.

Hitler nodded and smiled. "Yes, of course."

The rest of us looked at one another. Ribbentrop and Hitler obviously knew something we did not. So, with the approval of the German High Command (although he didn't need it, having appointed himself Commander in Chief of the Armed Forces), Hitler, on September 1, 1939, less than a month after confirming the Molotov-Ribbentrop Pact, marched into Poland.

When we expressed concern that this was a step too far in expansion, both Hitler and Ribbentrop laughed.

"I re-occupied the Ruhr that had been taken from us, and no one objected. I annexed Austria, and no one reacted. I broke off a large piece of Czechoslovakia, and Europe barely murmured. Then, a few months ago, I dismembered it completely, and there was no protest," Hitler said.

Ribbentrop shook his head. "You were all worrying for nothing. We know there will be the same response – mere whimpering from the likes of Great Britain and France – when our more than one million soldiers cross into Poland."

Again, we were silent. I did not look into the faces of my fellow cabinet members. I didn't have to, for I knew that all of us felt the same about Ribbentrop. His striking Aryan looks were in sharp contrast to all of us except for Himmler's second in command, Reinhard Heydrich; but, of course, Ribbentrop was simply lucky enough to be born tall, blond, and blue-eyed. No, it was his character that we all detested. He had married money, swindled his way into office by confiscating various Jewish businesses under our anti-Semite laws, and worst of all, bought his title '*von* Ribbentrop' by ingratiating himself with an aunt who adopted him – she, alone, could trace her ancestry back to nobility. As a businessman, he had traveled widely outside of Germany, and this experience, coupled with sheer flattery and boot-licking, gave him unparalleled access to Hitler, even more than mine or Göring's.

For example, Ribbentrop was astute enough to listen to Hitler's ideas and then, days later, reframe them and present them as his own back to the Führer, which Hitler misconstrued as brilliant concepts coming from an ideal diplomat for National Socialism. In short order, he became Hitler's choice for Germany's ambassador to the rest of the world. I made a mental note to watch Ribbentrop carefully.

I was thinking about how I could use my ministry to insinuate myself into the glorious victory that Hitler and Ribbentrop were now predicting. Or, conversely, how I could remain outside of the events in Poland, which I sensed would have far-reaching consequences not only for the Baltic states but for Germany, too.

"Hitler clicked his heels and bowed to Ribbentrop. "Your service to the Reich is noted. Your loyalty to me is appreciated. Soon, others," he paused and looked at all of us, "will show their loyalty as well, I'm sure."

Ribbentrop straightened his back and nodded. He glanced at the rest of us as if we were insignificant and then carelessly brushed a piece of lint from his left sleeve.

Once our discussion moved on to less significant matters, I decided to set my spies on Ribbentrop and Speer, both of whom were Hitler's current favorites. Of course, Adolf always loved my wife, Magda, and it was usually through her that I could win Hitler's attention anew. But I had to be careful. I did not think that war with Western Europe would be fruitful, at least not yet. To anger the likes of France and Britain might re-

sult in Germany paying a heavy price for its expansionist policies as had happened, I knew, in the last war. We had to tread
carefully, I thought, although I knew that Hitler believed he had
waited long enough.

With the entire country now mobilized for war, my job was merely to support that effort, always showing the best face of this new reality for Germany. On the one hand, I was surprised that we had conquered Western Europe so swiftly and easily with only England's stubborn resistance. On the other hand, I knew that my devotion to Hitler on account of his brilliant direction of this war. Adolf's Third Reich was indeed destined, as he predicted, to last for a thousand years.

By now, Magda and I had six children, the last having been born in 1940. Our marriage had weathered infidelities and differences of opinion, and now, married almost ten years, we had grown accustomed to one another, comfortable and secure in a relationship that made little or no demands on us.

"Why do you stay with me, Magda?" I asked one morning, still in bed.

Magda was sitting at her dressing table in a loose robe, brushing her hair. She did not turn to answer me but simply said to my reflection in her mirror, "Hitler would not have it otherwise." She said this as a matter of fact, without irony or regret.

"His opinion still means so much to you?"

"As it does to you, too, dear Joseph. It is, perhaps, more obvious in you with your never-ending schemes to publicly glorify him, but I still crave his approval as well." She shrugged her shoulders, again without irony or regret.

"I have simply assured that Germany recognizes him as I do: our savior. Now that we have conquered all of the Western European continent, I need to make sure that the Slavs, Nords, – all of them! – realize his greatness as well." Even if it was true that I was devoted more to Hitler than Germany, I hated to admit it publicly, as if it were a betrayal of my Aryan roots.

Magda turned towards me and folded her arms across her chest. "Why, Joseph? I wonder why you do this all for him? Why not apply your brilliant tactics to promoting yourself?"

I laughed. "Look at me, Magda. I am less than two meters tall, while most of the other ministers are more than two meters tall. I weigh a scant seventy-two kilograms. I am pale and thin-boned. And this," I pointed to my crippled leg, "is a poorly-kept secret. How does such a wreck promote itself as a savior?"

"So, you live vicariously through him? You make of him what you can never be yourself?"

"That is part of it, certainly," I said, "but there is more. I live in pain, Magda. Not just my leg but my soul. When I write, when I speak, when I act, I stand alone, unheralded, unappreciated. But when I put my words and my actions in him, the world sits up and takes notice."

"What you are saying is almost sacrilege," she answered. "You speak as if Hitler is merely the glittering container into which you pour yourself. He is your mask, your persona."

I hesitated before I answered, trying to decide if she was accusing me of a wrongdoing. "Yes, and think on it, Magda. You know that so much of what Hitler says and does derives from my suggestions, my prompts. It is *me*, Magda, but in a form more palatable to you, to all."

She stood up and untied her robe so that it hung loosely on either side of her still-taut and sensual body. "And here, in our bedroom?" she asked, moving toward me.

"Here, I am still afflicted with these physical weaknesses, but when I am pressed up against you, so close you cannot see my imperfections, all you will ever know is my ability to satisfy you, the skill rather than the appearance of my body to fulfill you. Isn't that so, Magda?" I lifted the sheet to invite her back into bed.

As the war continued to yield great victories for us, such as the British retreat at Dunkirk, I continued to urge Hitler to use history to our advantage. For example, at the end of the First World War, the French had humiliated us by having Germany sign the Treaty of Versailles in the Hall of Mirrors, the place where Germany had previously announced its empire. So, when France agreed to sign an armistice with us, we insisted it take place ironically at Compiègne, in the same railway car previously used to effect Germany's defeat. We would not just reverse the injustices of the past; we would use them to mock our enemies. Thus did I press Hitler to inflict pain on and exact retribution from those who opposed us.

I was constantly searching for new ways to present my propaganda for the National Socialist Party and, eventually, for Hitler himself. To reach all of the population, I made sure that, in celebration of my birthday, every home in Germany had a radio to hear Hitler's speeches. Knowing how adamant he was about his political views, I never questioned his policies or proposals. Instead, I coached him on presentation. "Sir, may I suggest that you use the pronoun 'I' instead of 'we'? You will thus insure that your listeners realize that you are the source of their resolution and salvation."

"Ah, *danke*, Joseph. Yes, only I can lead Germany to success."

"And begin your speeches with a hesitancy, as if you were putting forth an idea. Then, develop greater confidence by raising your volume, and end positively, with hope, as if saying a prayer you know will be answered."

"I think, Joseph, that even with audiences who do not understand me, they will be able to catch my meaning just by my tone and pitch." He cleared his throat.

"Please trust that I have studied your ideas and how they might be best presented." I was treading lightly, knowing that Adolf did not take well to criticism.

"And you obviously have some conclusions?" There was just a touch of annoyance in his comment.

"Suggestions, only, Sir. After all, only you can adequately judge your audience when you speak to them."

He stroked his mustache thoughtfully. "Yes, go on."

"I have noticed that you start your remarks with hesitancy, drawing your audience in to support and encourage you. Then, you begin to expound on your ideas. Here is where you have the opportunity to express rage on behalf of your listeners. *They* have been wronged by the Treaty of Versailles. *You* will remedy that because *you* are their champion. In short, you should move from grievance to rage to joy. Do you see how this works?"

Hitler grinned broadly and nodded. He did not need me to put the words in his mouth; he needed only for me to make his path clear.

"Finally, if I may, Sir." I bowed my head.

"Yes, more advice? Go ahead, Joseph. I trust your suggestions."

"You must show your appreciation of the crowd's approval. One of your signature gestures is to run your left hand through your hair as if making yourself presentable. It is, at once, a gesture of humility and respect. Do it when they are clapping for you or saluting you."

Hitler laughed. "I do it because my hair is sometimes unruly."

"Only we need to know that."

In addition, although Hitler's presence drew the most reaction from the crowds, I planned various events ostensibly to inform people of their government's activities but in reality to entertain people, to whet their appetites for more spectacle.

History helped me in this, for as much as we National Socialists wanted to tear down the traditional institutions that held us in thrall to an outdated past, we also understood that those institutions were our common heritage and imbued with significance for us. So, even as we promoted and urged modernity, we utilized traditions to attract people to us, in the same way that Hitler himself had realized that the best way to achieve power was to work within the structures of government itself before completely demolishing those structures.

Wherever I could, I imbued mass rallies with ceremonial and ritual elements. After all, Germany was filled with Teutonic mythology from which I could draw innumerable images and symbols. For example, there was the *Blutfahne*, the Blood Flag.

It was Adolf who first brought up the subject. "Do you know about vexillology, Joseph?"

When I did not immediately answer, he smiled broadly. "Ah, I have stumped the scholar!"

"I admit that despite my studies in philology, I do not know the term, *mein Führer*." Even in casual conversation, I liked him to know that I had only the utmost respect for him.

"It means 'the study of flags,' one of my recreational interests. Did you know that it was I who designed the flag of our party, the National Socialists?"

"I did not know, but I would, of course, never assume otherwise. You were, as I recall, once an artist in Vienna."

"Yes," Hitler said, but shaking his head as if shaking free of an unwanted memory. "I am sensitive to the meaning of colors and symbols."

I was already spinning in my head the various ceremonies I could conjure around our party flag.

"While I was imprisoned and writing *Mein Kampf*, I envisioned the design of our flag, Joseph, making sure to maintain our national colors of black, white, and red. I simply re-imagined them from three equal stripes to a red field on which I imposed a white circle and the *hakenkreuz* in black and at an angle. I wanted a more dramatic flag that would inspire Germany."

"I have read, of course, the very compelling work of Schliemann, the renowned anthropologist who first discovered the swastika in his digs for ancient Troy," I said, hoping to show Adolf that I knew *something* about symbols.

Hitler shook his finger at me. "*Nein*, Joseph, not the swastika, but the *hakenkreuz*, the hooked cross, is what I chose. It is not international but *Christian* in origin," he emphasized, "and, therefore," he concluded, "anathema to the Jews."

I nodded, recognizing that Adolf was shrewd enough to accept 'swastika' yet, when pressed, insist on 'hakenkreuz' as the more 'correct' term. "Very clever," I said. The Dionysus coin in my pocket suddenly seemed to burn, for I recognized for the first time that Hitler, like me, had sensed in himself some connection to the ancient past.

"I am, after all, a student of history, Joseph," he said and smiled. "And you shall help me to make this third Reich, under me, a historical age without equal." He straightened his back and squared his shoulders as if posing for a monument in his image.

I nodded in agreement and, not wanting the discussion to fade into abstractions, said, "I have an idea for the flag you designed. It is kept at the Munich Headquarters, yes?"

Hitler nodded. "It was the flag we carried at the Munich *putsch* of 1925, the first one we attempted, the first that failed because we acted too emotionally, the first where some of our compatriots died." He lowered his head and put his hand to his heart.

I could see that he was already rehearsing this moment to be part of one of his future speeches. "I think the flag can serve as more than an image in one of your speeches," I offered.

At the next Party Congress in Nuremberg, I made sure that each local office of National Socialism throughout Germany carried to the meeting a square banner with a design I had approved in advance. These were square red flags emblazoned with the hooked cross in a white circle. Printed on each banner were the words *Deutschland Erwache* – Germany Awake – and the banner itself, fringed in red, white, and black, was mounted on a metal pole topped with the imperial eagle standing on a wreath circling another hooked cross. Below that, I allowed a few variant slogans, the two most popular being the initials of the party (NSDAP) and the name of our Party's martyr, Horst Wessel. The variants, I explained to Hitler, were similar to the medieval ruler extending to his liege lords the privilege of administering local justice.

At the rally, the Munich flag – christened the *Blutfahne* – Blood Flag – was hoisted behind Hitler as he greeted each of the carriers of the local banners. The Blood Flag was not a mere symbol, for the blood of one Andreas Baureidl stained it after the young man, shot by the police during the unsuccessful *putsch*, fell onto the flag. His comrade, Heinrich Traumbauer, rescued the flag from the battle.

Hitler would grasp the Blood Flag in his left hand and, with his right hand, touch the corner of the local banner to the Munich standard, thereby imbuing it with the qualities of devotion, perseverance, and sacrifice. There were more than 400 local banners, so the ceremony took hours but never failed to inspire the attendees at Nuremberg. It was a symbolic Blood Oath for all concerned.

Moreover, it did not seem to exhaust Hitler. In fact, quite the contrary; he was energized each time he grasped a different banner and looked into the admiring face of the standard bearer. He almost seemed to grow in stature.

What I did not realize was that his vigor had grown, in large part, from his satisfaction with reports and suggestions he was receiving from Himmler and Reinhard Heydrich, the Chief of the Security Force. They were providing solutions to what Hitler considered his latest problem.

His anti-Semitism was not new, nor was his contention that the ultimate purpose of his war was to rid the world, once and for all, of the Jews. He should not have been surprised – although he was – when, in conquering Western Europe, he discovered that his "Jewish problem" had grown incrementally and was compounded by the existence of non-Jews who opposed him. His response was to require more incarceration sites throughout the new German empire.

I caught up with Heinrich Himmler one afternoon. "What's going on? I am getting reports from newspapers all over Germany and Austria that people are grumbling about prisons being built in their backyards."

Heinrich laughed scornfully. "Hardly prisons, Joseph. In

fact, we've established at least four kinds of camps – not prisons – as quickly as we can to handle the problem."

"And what do I tell the newspapers to allay the complaints of their readers?" I was annoyed that this was happening without my knowledge.

"I only have time to give you a quick response, Joseph. I'm so busy, and there are still adjustments that Hitler wants." He sighed. "So, first, these are camps. Not buildings with cells and bars and locks. More like barracks, but without any amenities. Conditions are harsh but livable. The concentration camps are for identified enemies of the Reich, the Jews, gypsies, and partisans. Forced labor camps contain able-bodied people to curtail our labor shortages caused by enlistments. Transit camps are temporary holding areas in our conquered territories to sort out the prisoners. Prisoner of war camps are for those enemy soldiers captured in combat. That's it. Our only worry is what to do with the overflow of prisoners as a result of our great victories."

I shook my head. "You're giving me only part of the picture, I'm sure. What of the feeble-minded, the terminally infirm?"

"Euthanasia. We are not socialists or communists. We will also euthanize those who can no longer serve as prisoners. We are not a charity state. We have enough trouble caring for the 25,000 or so that are now incarcerated."

"And the able-bodied?"

"They are set to work." He sighed again. "And when they are no longer useful, sometimes death, sometimes release, at least in the case of Germans."

"If released, they will reveal the cruel conditions. Better to eliminate them." I was thinking of how much of a publicity nightmare this could be.

"It is your job, Joseph, to publicize what we do and, at the same time, keep it a secret. Hitler demands this. Do you understand?"

"So, I must demonize these prisoners as degenerates, criminals, even race traitors."

"I knew you would find the right words, Joseph. I told Hitler that he could depend on you."

"Most are Jews, I presume."

"*That* is a distinct problem that we're considering. Without conclusion, I can say no more for now."

I nodded.

It was a Sunday – 22 June 1941, to be exact – when I heard the news. I was shaving in the bathroom of Trudi Haltzman, one of the researchers in my Film Department at the Ministry of Propaganda, while Trudi was fiddling with the radio.

"Tune to Berlin; they should be playing Beethoven this morning," I yelled to her as I wiped the last of the shaving cream from my face. "That whining and static is annoying."

"*Ich kann nicht,*" she explained.

Pulling my suspenders up over my shoulders, I went into the living room and took over the tuning dial. "Let me do it," I said, annoyed. "I don't have time for this. I'll be late for lunch with my family."

Trudi sat back in a sulk. She had been a pleasant enough dinner companion last evening and an acceptable bed partner last night, but this morning, I found her somewhat homely without her makeup and exhibiting the beginnings of that plump softness so typical of German *hausfraus*. Her slightly sour smell drove me to the bathroom, where I showered, reattached my leg brace, and put on my trousers.

Suddenly, the tail-end of an announcement crackled from the radio, " – as announced by the Ministry of War this morning at eight." Then, there was a brief burst of martial music.

"What the hell?" I muttered. "Trudi, my shirt and jacket, please," I said, snapping my fingers at her.

She darted obediently into the bedroom, emerging a moment later with my clothing heaped in her hands.

I called Himmler's home. His maid said he'd gone to the Ministry. I called his office.

"Himmler here. *Heil Hitler!*"

"Heinrich, what has happened? Radio Berlin says the War Office made some announcement, but I missed it." While I spoke, I finished dressing.

"Finally, Joseph! War with the Russian communists! We will crush them as we did everyone else." He didn't even try to moderate his delight.

"Do you have details?" I asked. I had to go to the Propaganda Ministry to prepare extensive press releases. I needed to assign media reporters, to send photographers with the troops. So much to do! I wouldn't be having lunch with the family after all.

"Göring knows more. I was only told that the attack is called Operation Barbarossa and it consists of three million troops. I have to go, Joseph, much to do now." He hung up.

I stared at the phone for a moment, then dialed Magda. "If you've heard the news, you know that I won't be having lunch with you and the children," I said as soon as she answered.

"Where are you now?" Magda asked.

"I'll be in my office most of the day. If things go wrong, into the night as well."

"So I would assume. Where are you now?" she repeated.

I ignored her question, not wanting to start an argument about my whereabouts. "Can you bring fresh clothes to my office after lunch today?"

Magda cleared her throat and spoke quietly. "Yes, of course. Will you want someone to bring some lunch as well?"

I realized that she would send one of the servants, not come herself. "I would like to see *you*, Magda."

"As you know, Joseph, I always spend Sunday afternoons with the children. They so look forward to my company."

"Yes, of course," I conceded. I would have to answer Magda's accusations of my suspected infidelity later tonight. When I hung up, I turned to Trudi. "Get dressed and call my secretary. Tell her to call everyone. I'll be having a full office meeting in three hours." I started to lace my shoes. "Be a sweetheart and run downstairs to wake my driver. Tell him I'll be down in fifteen minutes. Thank you, Trudi."

When I arrived at my office, I could see that the lights in Hitler's building across the square were already lit up. People and cars arrived steadily. I sat back in my chair at my desk. I was already planning on who I would send to record in photos and on film our invasion of Russia, and what press releases I would send out via telegram to the German newspapers. Other news outlets outside of Germany would accept no press releases from me unless they were simple facts: who, when, where, what, and how. I would be unable to convince them to print stories that asserted our invasion to be a necessary action to contain Russian communism and prevent its spread throughout Europe, even though those assertions were true. The Western Europeans would only see that we, the Germans, were the aggressors, the breakers of our 1939 treaty with Russia.

As the members of my ministry arrived, I simply told them to stay on the telephones, to call whomever they could, to glean any and all information about the invasion, noting the source of the information as well as commenting on its reliability. No one was to leave until I decreed the crisis to be over.

Annoyed that neither nourishment nor a change of clothes had appeared in my offices by two p.m., I called Magda. "Where is the damned servant with my things, Magda?"

"I decided to bring everything myself, but I am settling the children with the nanny and waiting for your meal to be prepared. I'll be there in an hour."

"Send the maid," I answered, not wanting a discussion with Magda about where I was last night or why my clothes smelled of perfume.

"No, I insist as your devoted wife," she said sarcastically.

Magda brought me a thin soup and some bread as well as a full change of clothes.

"Well, thank you, my wife, for the clothes," I said, preparing to change right there in my office. "But the nourishment is rather paltry." I made a face.

"I expect you to take me somewhere for a nice dinner and drinks, Joseph. I haven't seen you since yesterday morning. What would Adolf say if he knew you were neglecting me?"

I shook my head. "Don't you see that he has more pressing problems right now?" I had stripped down to my underwear, socks, and brace. I sat in my chair.

"Please, Joseph, get dressed." Magda wrinkled her nose in disgust.

"Lock the door, Magda," I said. "And draw the curtains." I remained still in my chair. "Then, remove your dress."

"What is this ridiculous game?" she asked. There was a tremor of fear and excitement in her voice.

"I would do this in our bed at home, but I cannot leave the office at this crucial time. So, it has to be done here."

"What are you talking about?" She remained standing in her clothes.

"Haven't you noticed that we are really only honest with each other when we are naked in bed? This must be a moment of honesty for us, Magda, please."

She hesitated only a moment, then turned and locked the door, walked to the windows and drew the heavy drapes closed, and then removed her dress, letting it drop to the floor. She moved to the leather couch against the wall. "At least, let us be somewhat comfortable," she said. "Turn off the lights and come to me, Joseph."

I left the desk lamp burning but switched off the overhead lights and went to Magda on the couch, where we both undressed and lay next to one another. The room was in deep shadows except at my desk. "Shall we make love?" I asked, embracing her.

"At least you had the decency to shower off the stink of

that other woman, whoever she might have been." Magda embraced me back.

To me, and I think to Magda as well, our love-making was gentle, almost timid, recalling our first days together when we were unfamiliar with each other's desires. After, I lit two cigarettes, and we lay quietly against one another on that narrow couch. "Do you know why I've wanted this?" My voice sounded small and simple in the dark.

"So I would forgive or forget your infidelity?" Magda asked. Her voice, too, was disembodied as if appearing out of nowhere.

"No, because I think that this war Hitler has unleashed will change us all. I wanted this last experience with you, the Magda I knew from before this day."

"You are being melodramatic, Joseph."

"No, listen to me. Nothing will be the same after this, Magda, I am sure of it. You know," I said, hugging her closer, "I have always loved you and the children."

"And why would that change?"

"Because the world will change, and nothing can remain in such a great shift."

What is this 'great shift' you speak about as if it were some mystical thing?" Magda turned to rest her head on my chest.

"I don't know what its outcome will be, Magda. I only know that nothing will remain the same. There are only two things that could happen: Germany will conquer Russia and rid the world of Jews, or Germany will be defeated, and the Jews will win the world. It is that simple, that stark."

"Nonsense, Joseph. We have already taken over Western Europe. Russia will be the same, only in the opposite direction."

"I hope that with all my heart. But hope does not guarantee success. Besides, Magda, you are forgetting that England still resists us."

"They cannot sustain that against our superior forces."

"They've proven strong adversaries so far. If the Americans enter the war, British resolve will be strengthened even further. Moreover, to fight the Russians, we must move much of our army to the Eastern Front. And now what? – war at our front *and* our back. It is the way we lost the last war, I fear."

Magda let her cigarette burn down to near her fingers, then she got up and stubbed it out in the ashtray on my desk. She retrieved her clothes. "Say nothing like this to the others or to Adolf. You would be putting me and the children in danger," she whispered in the dark.

"Turn on the lights," I said. I heard her pad across the floor in the dark, and the lights suddenly came on. I sat up and dressed. "Never," I promised. "I will be Adolf's most faithful advocate. And Magda," I added, "I will try to never be unfaithful to our marriage again." I hoped she saw that vow as an expression of my earnestness in this entire conversation.

"Is fear of defeat the cause for your sudden conversion?" she asked, almost laughing.

"Only partially," I answered. I reached into my pocket and tossed the coin she had given me so long ago onto my desk. It clattered there for a few seconds, then fell flat and silent.

"That antique? You still carry it?" She touched its surface but did not pick it up.

"It reminds me of what I owe to my prior lives."

"What do you mean, what you owe? An obligation?"

"Yes. Don't you see, Magda. Me, this life, it is nothing more than a rebirth, a spirit being born again in another time and place. My body is simply the receptacle for that spirit."

"This is some arcane nonsense that has been put in your head by your reading too many books, Joseph." Magda snorted.

"No, I would wish it were mere drivel, but I have had my lifetime to see that it is not. My nightmares become sharper and clearer each year. That, and my studies in Dionysian cults and rituals, convince me that I – or rather, my spirit – has lived at least twice before and will probably live again."

"Even if rebirth were true, there are no records, no scientific proofs that demonstrate reincarnation to be true. More, no one has ever had more than a vague hunch about a previous life. These are like fairy tales invented by Jakob Grimm."

"When I can tolerate it, I allow my nightmares to reveal intricate details of my previous lives, but more than facts of existence, they show me the nature of my spirit in each life, how that spirit developed, existed, and then escaped the body to seek another host."

"Now you are talking as if some alien thing moves from human body to human body for its own purposes." Magda shook her head.

"I will not tell you about the life of Father Malcolm Murray or Friar Diego de Herrerra. I will not describe to you their environments of Scotland or the Philippines. You would only think me a vivid storyteller. I will simply explain the spirit that drove them." I rubbed my face, tired and heavy with what I knew.

"You look pale and exhausted. Why not just rest?"

"I need to share this with someone, with *you*, Magda, because we share a life together, six children, and love for the same person. We have settled for one another, Magda, and now you will see who you have thrown in with at last." I waited a moment, but she said nothing.

"Magda, the spirit that is me, that gives me life, is one of immense lust. In the Scotsman Malcolm it expressed itself in excessive sexual acts and unrestrained behavior in carnality. And because the spirit lacked moderation, the man was physically marked with an evil eye and a clubfoot. He died violently, torn apart by those incensed with his behavior. When the spirit found another body, it was in the Spaniard Diego, who was excessively devout, developing a masochism arising from his belief that only through physical pain could he experience spiritual pleasure. He lacked normal sexual organs. He, too, in that overbearing devotion that he preached to others, was killed by those who believed his missionary work would destroy their beliefs. And when that body was murdered, the spirit escaped to find yet another host."

"You?" Magda whispered, entranced by the story.

"Yes, me. The cripple." I put my hand over my eyes.

"And what is your excess, Joseph?"

"I am not sure yet, Magda, but I suspect it has something to do with my admiration for Adolf Hitler." I would not look at her.

Magda shook her head. "You are overwrought. I insist we go out for dinner and drinks, forget about this whole Russia thing until tomorrow, and go home, kiss our children, and go to bed. You will not feel this burden in the morning, Joseph."

I nodded, surrendering to her suggestions, but I knew the burden would remain in the morning and that, in fact, even with Magda beside me, the nightmares would return, but this time not to torment me but to reassure me that everything I had said was true.

Final Resolve

When I looked back, the invasion of Russia on that Sunday in June was the longest day of the war as well as the longest day of the year, the summer solstice. It was also the key turning point in Magda's and my marriage.

We agreed on that day that we would never make love again, thereby assuring that we would have no more children. A calm acceptance came over us after so many years of bickering, uncertainties, and infidelities. We did not promise celibacy exactly, however, just a greater discretion in dealing with temporary sexual partners; we promised each other that we would keep our private lives confidential and hidden from Adolf.

He was, thankfully, preoccupied with the conquest of Russia. Although our victory over that vast land would mean an increased problem with those who opposed us, Hitler insisted that our defeat of the Bolsheviks and communism was paramount, taking precedence over any other concerns of the Reich. It was, he said, our destiny to enact the defeat of worldwide Jewry.

In fact, he had chosen to code-name the initial invasion of Russia "Operation Barbarossa" after Frederick Barbarossa, a twelfth-century German Emperor and Crusader. Frederick was known as *Kaiser Rotbart* (Emperor Redbeard) in Germany but derived his nickname from Italian (*barbarossa* meaning 'red beard') because of his campaigns in Northern Italy. Frederick was described by his contemporaries as almost godlike in his abilities both in battle and in politics, and Hitler suggested that he was Frederick's modern successor.

Victory over Russia would mean the fulfillment of Hitler's policy of *Lebensraum* (living space) for Germany. Western Russia would be repopulated with Germans while the conquered people would be used in forced labor for Germany's war efforts. Eventually, the native Slavs could be enslaved and sent to Siberia to perish, while the Jews would be killed on the spot. Hitler's *blitzkrieg* had worked in Western Europe, and it seemed destined to be successful in the Russian campaign as well.

Despite my misgivings about a two-front war, all of my time was now devoted to glorifying the conflict. There was no aspect of German life that I did not imbue with patriotic propaganda in order to keep the civilian population informed but also enthusiastic, as well as to support the troops who were being sent far afield to Gibraltar in the west, North Africa to the south, and to the Soviet Union in the East. Hitler trusted me to be his spokesman to the people while he oversaw the direction of the war.

In addition, my prior concerns about the proliferation of concentration camps throughout Germany were partially allayed by Himmler's quick thinking and the efficiency of his first-in-command, Reinhard Heydrich. Initially, those in conquered territories who opposed us were shipped by train to camps in Germany for imprisonment. This strained local resources for food and safety, in addition to using up transportation lines needed for the war effort. Himmler's idea was the establishment of *Einsatzgruppen* – task forces – to deal with the opposition swiftly and efficiently.

The task force would gather undesirable civilians in the conquered territories, march them to an isolated area, and shoot them. These civilians were first, those most likely to voice opposition to us, the so-called *intelligentsia*, then the cultural elite of a country, then those religious leaders (such as many of the Catholic priesthood in Poland), followed by political leaders, Jews, partisans, and gypsies. Such swift justice freed up the trains to transport armaments and our troops and also negated the need to further supply the camps.

"You look better, Joseph," Magda said to me one night while we ate dinner with the children.

"I am much relieved, Magda," I answered, patting her hand. "I was worried about a two-front war, but that is proving baseless. I was worried about the logistics of a large, unruly population of conquered people, but Himmler provided a solution. My job is simply to explain how easily and efficiently our Third

Reich can operate."

"And no worries?" she asked, smiling.

"Adolf is pleased, which means everything is good. An end to war, I am assured by the generals, is on the horizon. Once Russia is subdued, we will turn our attention back to Britain and crush that little island mercilessly."

"And the Americans?" Magda asked, knowing we had all carefully watched how that country was reacting to our decisions.

"We've been fighting the Russians for three months, Magda, and are now headed to take over their capital, Moscow. Before Christmas, we will have established our rule over the communists. The Americans remain silent, unwilling to cross the ocean for their allies."

"And, then, Joseph, what of us?" Magda asked quietly. I realized that she had been leading up to this all along.

"Aren't we settled, Magda? We have our family to raise. We accept that neither of us loves the other as much as we both love Adolf. Our lives are comfortable and secure."

"You sound like the capitalists you once despised," Magda observed.

"I have moderated my opinion of capitalism now that it serves us. We have numerous apartments here in Berlin, other homes in the best neighborhoods and suburbs, cars, and servants. We go where we want, eat what we want, and – discreetly, as agreed – sleep with whomever we want. I have taken all the hatred I had for capitalism and put it toward my hatred of Jews and communists, finding that they are often the same for me."

"You seem to have no more room for love, either. Perhaps hatred is your excess," Magda concluded sadly.

"I love Adolf. That will never change. The rest of my life is fueled by hate and the satisfaction of pleasing the Führer." I touched Magda's arm. "And you have spent days, even weeks, Magda, at Adolf's side, seeming to forget you have a family here."

"At least half the time, the children come with me to stay at Adolf's place. They enjoy time with their Uncle as much as I do," Magda argued. "Besides, I doubt you are ever alone more than two consecutive nights." She laughed. "And before you ask if I am jealous, be assured I am not, Joseph. I am simply stating the reality. I almost admire your stamina."

I nodded. "We have done well, Magda. We should both be happy."

"Nevertheless, Joseph, I want you to think about this: in all your propaganda, do you not think it better to convert people to your point of view rather than to destroy them?"

"Perhaps for some, Magda, but for the Jews? They will never be other than Jews, so conversion is not an option." I shook my head. "We must kill them all, and if we run out of bullets, we must find another way to be rid of them once and for all."

Magda shrugged her shoulders. "If that is what you and Adolf wish."

However, as I had known all my life but sometimes forgot, what we wish is not always what comes to pass. The war with Russia was not the *blitzkrieg* Hitler and his generals had predicted. The swift advances they made only served to stretch thin their line of offense, thereby weakening them and slowing their forward movement. This, in turn, gave the communists more time to fortify their own defenses as well as to mount an offensive. Six months after the Barbarossa Operation, we found ourselves stopped at the Battle of Moscow in December. Then, in the harsh Soviet winter at the beginning of 1942, we were unable to hold our lines and were pushed back more than one hundred miles. Our retreat continued through 1942, despite Hitler's insistence that we stay the course. On several occasions, I pleaded with him to reconsider the attack on Russia, for we had already killed over three million Soviet fighters and a million Soviet Jews; we could pull back, I argued, and rebuild our forces. Each time, he refused to change his plans, insisting that his vision was clear and correct. And each time, he scowled at me and demanded I apologize.

Of course, I conceded. And I started to frame the news reports in terms that made our losses seem trivial. This also became true for our battles on the Western Front, for America joined the war as a result of the Japanese attack on Pearl Harbor in 1941. They, too, were fighting the war on two fronts, but realizing that their war with Japan would be prolonged and difficult, they decided to first help the Western European nations make quick work of their war with us, thereby committing most of their energy to the Allied forces.

Of course, this strained our resources to a breaking point, already diminished because of the need on the Eastern front. Himmler and his people were lauded for finding an efficient alternative to shooting the enemies of Germany: gas chambers were set up at various camps, and incinerators were built to dispose of the bodies. When explaining this development to us, the cabinet, he said, "We saved ammunition for our soldiers. Besides, we couldn't bury the bodies fast enough."

On New Year's Day in 1943, I took Magda to a night on the town. There had been some British attempts at bombing the city, but these were ineffectual and infrequent. The city was still the heartbeat of the new Germany, the Third Reich.

"Are we celebrating anything special?" Magda asked as she opened the menu. I'd made the reservation here at Horcher's because I knew she enjoyed their vichyssoise.

"Probably our last meal out in Berlin for a while," I said.

"What?" Magda seemed truly shocked.

"We'll be eating only at home by next month, probably," I explained.

"But why?" Magda closed her menu and shooed away the waiter. She leaned in toward me.

"I am closing all non-essential businesses in Germany, starting with Berlin."

"Joseph, that is not good propaganda."

"I will make it so, Magda. Don't worry." I opened my napkin and placed it on my lap. "So, let's enjoy this night out, shall we?" I did not tell her that orders were being sent to Russia to dig in after the commander-in-chief there, Friedrich Paulus, wired Berlin that he intended to surrender. For me, the surrender meant a hard time ahead.

"How are your nightmares?"

"Still my companions when I am alone, sometimes even when I am with a woman." I shrugged.

"But never when I was with you, Joseph," Magda stated.

"Perhaps that is the impossible solution, dear."

The following month, on February 18th, I made my speech at the Berlin *Sportpalast*. I had selected my audience of over 14,000 as boosters of my ideas, because I was also broadcasting my remarks on the radio to millions more Germans. I had gained Adolf's approval for the speech after I explained to him that it was meant to inform the people of the progress of our war and to elicit their further support. In fact, I believed the speech to be necessary propaganda after Paulus had surrendered the entire German 6th Army to the Soviets at the Battle of Stalingrad. Worse, although Adolf expected it, Paulus did not take his own life after the surrender, choosing instead to be taken prisoner and held in Soviet captivity.

But I intended my speech to be the basis for Adolf awarding me some new recognition. I was bored with the Ministry of Propaganda and noted that Himmler, in particular, was being elevated in status almost every day. There was gossip that he was to be made Reichminister of the Interior, a post that I coveted and believed would mesh perfectly with my Propaganda Ministry. I needed to outdo him in Adolf's eyes.

As planned, my speech not only inspired all of Germany but also gained the admiration of Adolf, particularly when I called for "total war" against the "cabal of globalists and Jews."

I did not shrink from our setbacks, noting they were "misfortunes of the past weeks," and I assured my audience that I was presenting an "unvarnished picture of the situation." I propagandized elegantly; that is, I did not lie. I simply omitted some of the harder truths: we were losing North Africa, and Churchill and Roosevelt were demanding our unconditional surrender. I urged my audience to "Let the storm break loose!" which was a call to mobilize on the home front, a campaign designed by Hitler to prolong the war for at least a year until fate turned back in our favor. He was determined that if we would not win, we would at least never recapitulate as Germany had done in 1918.

The campaign underscored the idea that Germany was the only bulwark that stood between Soviet Bolshevism and Western Europe. I called for severe austerity measures: conscripting citizens for war-related labor, closing more than 100,000 clubs and restaurants throughout Germany, the latter including Horcher's, a Berlin café since 1904, where Magda and I had our last wartime night out, and urging all to sacrifice for Germany, for the Führer, to show to the world that we were like a victorious storm let loose upon our enemies.

Some in the cabinet faltered in these terrible years of the early forties; some had been with Hitler since the first putsch in Munich, and I wondered if the old saying were true for them: familiarity breeds contempt. However, I ultimately believed them to be nothing more than cowards and traitors. Had they supported Adolf only to enrich themselves? Were they now, in this moment of temporary faltering of National Socialism, too ready to abandon our cause? I became more careful with others, suspicious of motives, and less likely to engage in open disagreement. I quietly warned Magda to be even more discreet.

"I am hearing, Joseph," she confided, "that many in Adolf's cabinet are preparing for eventualities other than victory. You must take note."

Our worst fears were realized in July 1944 when we learned of the attempt to assassinate Adolf at Wolf's Lair, his headquarters outside of Berlin, for the war with Russia. When that plot failed, retribution was swift, just as during the Night of the Long Knives: within months, almost five thousand people were executed, two hundred of them confirmed conspirators in the assassination attempt.

"Where was your silver tongue, Joseph?" Adolf demanded.

"With your permission, my Führer," I explained, "most of the conspirators were members of the army, the *Wehrmacht*, not loyal German citizens. Look to those who oversee the armed forces."

"Steps have already been taken," he answered coldly.

Desperate to prove my devotion, I said, "May I suggest that every member of the *Wehrmacht* be required to swear a loyalty oath to you, by name, rather than simply to *Deutschland*. Also, add the salutation *Heil Hitler* to the new military greeting, which we shall call the 'Hitler Salute.'"

Hitler knitted his brows in thought for a moment, then smiled. "Good work, Joseph, good work, indeed."

I breathed a sigh but continued to smile. I would not display my alarm with the near success of the latest assassination nor with Adolf's mercurial changes of temper.

Party

Throughout the latter part of 1944, the fortunes of Germany continued to decline. I reached back into history to find a parallel sweep of events which finally resolved themselves into victory for the presumed loser because I wanted to support Adolf's decision to keep fighting. I had to discount victories by the English or French because they were our enemies, and any mention of their good fortune would send Adolf into a furious ire.

"We will prevail, Sir, as the Hungarians did during the siege of Eger in the sixteenth century," I assured him as he mulled over his daily battle reports.

"As I recall, they were fighting the Ottomans," Adolf commented absently.

"Yes, outnumbered seventeen to one, enduring heavy casualties, but victorious after more than a month of assaults."

Tapping on the sheaf of battle reports in his hand, Adolf replied, "Anyone can deal with victory. Only the mighty can bear defeat."

I bowed and left the room.

Adolf was persuaded to move into the Führerbunker in January 1945. He seemed reluctant to do so, but I noticed a certain relief when the suggestion was made to him. The attempted assassination at Wolf's Lair six months earlier had not succeeded, but only by chance, Hesse told me, snickering. The traitor, Army officer Claus von Stauffenberg, had brought an attaché case filled with explosives to a meeting and left the case under the table where Hitler was standing. Stauffenberg discreetly left, and another officer thoughtlessly moved the case so that when it exploded, Hitler himself was shielded by a table leg. Even so, both his eardrums were punctured, and he suffered superficial wounds; weeks later, he was still bleeding from various cuts, and he suffered some dizziness and loss of balance. His doctor, Theodor Morell, treated him with a variety of drugs and potions.

Reminding Hitler of that incident allowed his cabinet to convince him that he must, for the good of Germany, repair to the bunker near the Chancellery in Berlin. That bunker, designed by my protégé Albert Speer, actually consisted of two separate but connected underground fortifications: the upper chamber, called the *Vorbunker*, had actually been completed as an air raid shelter three years before we marched into Poland, and the *Führerbunker*, dug deeper and more fortified than the first. Hitler's rooms were in the lower, safer section and made comfortable by self-contained water, communications, and electrical systems. Before he would agree to relocate there, he ordered Magda to oversee the installation of furnishings and décor because, he told her, "You have impeccable taste."

While Magda occupied herself with choosing furniture and accessories for Hitler and enduring the wrath of his girlfriend, Eva Braun, who felt slighted on this occasion, I was watching the steady losses our forces suffered under the onslaught of the Allied forces led by Churchill of Great Britain, Roosevelt of the United States, and Stalin of the Soviet Union. It seemed to me that the British supplied the courage, the Americans the armaments, and the Russians the manpower; we could not compete. My faith in Adolf's wisdom was beginning to falter, although I never expressed this doubt, not even to Magda.

Until the following month. Over a period of three days, February 13 to 15, 1945, the Allied forces – the British and Americans primarily – fire-bombed Dresden. The seventh-largest city in Germany, known for its delicate, ornate porcelain, had become a crossroads of the war, threatened primarily by the advancing Soviet ground forces. However, in that three-day period, British and American planes pounded this once gentle city (described as "Florence on the Elbe River") with what was described as "terror bombing," a tactic designed to overwhelm civilian services, particularly transportation, and create masses of refugees.

Dresden was not prepared because they had not been previously attacked during the war. The weather that February was windy, and the bombs that were dropped, including numerous incendiaries, created firestorms that almost instantaneously incinerated tens of thousands of people. At the end of the three days, around 25,000 inhabitants had died, and more undocumented deaths probably occurred, given the influx of thousands of refugees fleeing the Eastern Front. Most of the victims were women, children, and the elderly.

When I received the reports about Dresden, I locked my office door, closed the heavy drapes, and wept at my desk. I was filled with anguish for those terrible deaths, but I was also angry that Dresden was not spared like Rome, the seat of Mussolini's power. Moreover, Dresden contained relatively few military or strategic targets, and it seemed that the high casualty rate was meant simply as a cruel lesson. Bombing was bad enough, but razing the city with phosphorus bombs that burned everything to ash was ruthless.

The event erased any doubts I had about Adolf or his goals. Our enemies, I realized, did not want us merely defeated; they wanted us expunged from the earth. This war had led to a binary choice: us or them. There was no middle ground, no compromise, no bargaining. Adolf, I saw, was right: we win, or we die.

Meanwhile, I railed against those in the party who could not see the truth. First, of course, was Hermann Göring, whose Luftwaffe had failed again: they had been unable to bring Great Britain to its knees, and they had not defended the skies over Dresden.

I dialed his number. "Hermann!" I exclaimed as soon as he answered.

He recognized my voice. "Yes, Joseph, are you calling to scold me in Hitler's name?" His scorn was evident.

"Have you no compassion?" I sputtered. "Where was your vaulted Luftwaffe while Dresden burned?"

"Your fight is done with words, Joseph. Mine with actual armaments, which we hardly have, and petrol, which puts our planes in the air. We must choose our battles, Joseph, and choose only those we expect to win."

"Total war, Göring, *total war*. That means you fight *all* battles."

"Where there is much to lose, one must decide how best to survive. You are not a military man. How could you understand?" And, abruptly, he hung up.

I thought for an instant to call him back, then to report him to Adolf. But I decided to cool down a bit. Göring sounded like he was having second thoughts about the war, but without concrete evidence, I would not risk upsetting the lines of command at this crucial time. Wait and see, I told myself.

After Dresden, Adolf changed. Perhaps it was a result of having to live in the dreary environment of the bunker, but he was visibly different. Magda had done whatever she could to make the bunker comfortable and even homely. Aside from transporting some of the elegant furniture from the Chancellery, she ordered the walls be decorated with framed paintings and the lights be set to simulate daylight. Even so, Adolf seemed diminished in the bunker.

When I met privately with him at the beginning of March, I was alarmed by the physical changes in him. He had become slightly stooped and developed a shuffle in his walk. His complexion was waxy, his hair dull, and his eyes glassy. "Morell has me on vitamins and energy tonics to counteract this gloomy atmosphere," Adolf said to me when he saw the concern in my eyes. "And it is difficult to sleep these days."

"Understandable," I muttered and lowered my eyes to conceal my anxiety. I had handed Adolf a document, and when he reached out to receive it, his hands were visibly shaking.

He immediately placed the page on the table and clasped his hands behind his back. "I'll read that later, Joseph. What have you to report?" He found a seat in a large armchair in the corner.

"I regret to report that as a result of the failure of the Ardennes Offensive, our ground forces are in a slow retreat from many of the territories we had conquered," I started in a low voice.

"It is not my fault, Joseph," Adolf murmured. He closed his eyes. "Continue."

"Göring's Luftwaffe is also severely crippled as a result of the failed offensive, so our air defenses are compromised."

Adolf laughed sardonically. "That is not news. The bunker shakes with the continual Allied bombings."

"Yet," I said, clearing my throat, "we persist. And, the good news is that we are preparing a wonderful birthday for you in April. The bunker will be filled with music and celebration, I assure you." I stood up to leave, hoping that I had cheered Adolf somewhat.

Adolf rose clumsily. With an uncharacteristic warmth, he touched my cheek and said, "You and Magda sustain me." Then, he added, "Tomorrow, you will receive the details of a decree I have sent to Speer. It will be your duty to present it to the people as an act of heroism for Germany."

The next day, I saw the order titled "Decree Concerning Demolitions in the Reich Territory." To be carried out under the direction of Albert Speer, it ordered the destruction of Germany's infrastructure before it could be taken by the Allies; this included all transportation and communications facilities, industrial sites, and supply depots. It meant that nothing should be left intact. It was Hitler's response to the Allies' insistence on our unconditional surrender: he would not repeat what he considered the shame of the 1918 Treaty of Versailles.

That is, in 1918, when Germany surrendered, all of its resources were taken over by the conquering French and British. But now, Hitler decided, the Allied victory would be diminished by Germany's destruction of its own resources: nothing of value would be left to confiscate.

I thought back to how he had touched my cheek and wondered what that gesture had meant. Was it like his decree which, I suspected, was his way of indicating that the German people had failed him, that they proved unworthy of his great mission in history, that when his glorious Third Reich perished, so would they? Had I failed him? My heart sank. I had to correct this error.

I called Speer. "Do as his decree dictates, Albert. He is our Führer." I had brought Speer into the inner circle. He was my protégé and had, in some respects, managed to be more favored than I in Adolf's eyes. Yet, I wasn't jealous; I felt like I had simply brought Adolf another advocate.

"I will do what is appropriate," Speer said mysteriously.

The next day, Martin Bormann, Hitler's personal secretary, called my ministry to ask me to provide a cameraman that afternoon in the garden of the bunker; Adolf was going outside. Bormann added, "It is becoming dangerous. This may be the last time the Führer leaves the bunker for a while."

I immediately complied, sending my best man. I met the fellow as soon as he returned. "So, what was the occasion?" I asked.

"The Führer was awarding medals to a Hitler Youth group of about fifteen boys."

"How did it go?"

"Happily, the bombs were falling some distance away, so we were not in danger, although the sound was disconcerting. The boys seemed uncomfortable, however, given the circumstances." The cameraman shrugged. "As soon as I've developed the film and done a little editing, I'll set it up in the screening room for you."

The silent film was no longer than ten minutes. It opened with Hitler emerging from the bunker dressed in a heavy overcoat, his cap characteristically pulled low on his forehead. Two still photos were inserted at the opening of the film: Hitler standing with his adjutant in the ruins of the Chancellery that Hitler himself had designed. Then, he was smiling, confident, as he strode forward to a line of young boys, all standing at attention but clearly nervous and ill at ease. None seemed older than thirteen or so, and all were dressed as Hitler in overcoats. Most were without hats, their hair unkempt and standing in cowlicks on their heads. Hitler walked down the line, and within a few seconds, his smile faded, his gait slowed, and his posture slumped. He stopped at one of the shorter boys, turned to smile briefly at the camera, and then pinched the boy's cheek fondly. He said something to the boy. As the camera panned back for a wide-angle shot, it revealed Hitler's left hand tucked behind his back. For some reason, the cameraman panned in, and we clearly saw the left arm trembling uncontrollably. When the shot returned to a closeup of Hitler and the boy, Adolf patted the boy's cheek as he would pat the head of one of his dogs before he moved on.

When the film finished, I sat in the darkroom for a moment longer, reviewing the film in my mind. I decided I would only release it after some careful editing. In my hands, it would show the people Hitler's compassion for them.

Although Adolf and Eva had already moved their residence into the bunker, Hitler waited until April 1st to move his military headquarters into the upper section. It was a bitter acknowledgement of the dangerous situation. Meanwhile, I had charged Magda with preparing the festivities for Adolf's birthday on the twentieth of the month; he was to celebrate his 56th birthday.

I decided that my ministry was unable to continue providing war news to the people; there were no victories to report after all. Instead, in keeping with Hitler's orders to fight on, I decided that the public should be encouraged to demonstrate their courage and determination in the face of such overwhelming odds. For example, the Berlin Philharmonic gave a performance in Berlin to a full house of military and political elites. Among other pieces, they performed Brünnhilde's last aria and the finale from Wagner's *Götterdämmerung*, and at the conclusion of the concert, a contingent of Hitler Youth provided cyanide capsules to the departing audience.

Magda was informed only two days earlier that there was to be no birthday party in the bunker. Hitler, she was told, was not feeling well and needed rest, according to his doctor's orders. She could not convince Martin Bormann to persuade his boss to allow the celebrations to go forward.

Both his military command and us, his cabinet, were called to the bunker in the early evening for a conference. We were informed that the Soviets were expected to break through the lines and to be in Berlin soon. We all urged Hitler to depart, but he adamantly refused. He stated that he would never leave Berlin. A hush fell over the group, no one willing to argue with him, for despite his grey pallor and trembling hands, his eyes and mouth were set hard and unyielding.

Then, Eva Braun appeared in the doorway of the conference room. "Adolf, I know you forbade it, but I could not resist," she said impishly. "There are cakes and drinks in our quarters for everyone. We simply must celebrate your birthday."

There was some nervous laughter. Then, Hitler smiled and said softly, "My lovely Eva never fails to raise my spirits. Come, gentlemen." He rose and we all followed him down the concrete staircase to the lower bunker. Except Göring, who hung back.

"I'm sorry," he said, "but the news forces me to attend to the placement and activities of the Luftwaffe. I have a long drive ahead; I must leave immediately." He bowed to Hitler, saluted, and exited the bunker without waiting for approval.

I found Magda there standing in a corner. "When Eva heard about the cancellation, she called me and we arranged this secretly." She winked. "Desperate measures for desperate times."

But the party was heavily subdued and by eleven p.m., Eva declared that Adolf needed his rest and shooed us all out.

Magda and I locked arms. "We must talk," I said as we trudged back up the staircase and out into the night to our waiting car.

Götterdämmerung

We rode in silence to our estate on Schwanenwerder Island in southwestern Berlin. Most of the bombing was north and east of us in the industrial and commercial sectors. Once the car crossed the small bridge, we relaxed more, assured of our safety for the night.

"Tomorrow we pack, Magda. You and the children must join me permanently in the bunker." I did not look at her.

"What of the other cabinet ministers and their families?" she asked.

I waved my hand, indicating to her that I did not wish to speak about the matter in the car and within earshot of the driver. "Everyone is accounted for," I said noncommittally as the car pulled into the breezeway. "Let's get some sleep."

In the house, which I'd easily acquired in the thirties when we began restricting Jewish ownerships, we instructed the staff to prepare the children for a move the next day or the day after; we assured the servants that they could remain in our home until the danger from the Allies passed. We were moving the children only "as a precaution."

Alone, Magda and I sat in the large kitchen with two candles burning. It was almost one a.m., and the whine of the bombs and sirens could be heard only faintly, interspersed with the nearer occasional sound of a heron or a bullfrog in the Havel River. "How serious is this, Joseph?" Magda asked.

"Quite, I'm afraid, Magda," I answered truthfully. "The Soviets are on the outskirts of Berlin, driving down from the north. When we urged Hitler to escape south, he categorically refused, then immediately launched into a diatribe about those in government and the military who had betrayed him. He stopped only when Eva appeared and announced that she had prepared a small party for his birthday."

"I noticed his pallor. The turn of events in this war has clearly affected him," Magda said with concern.

"He has been declining ever since the retreat from Moscow started. It only worsens, and that quack doctor of his, Morrel, simply fills him with potions and pills rather than attempting any real cure. Adolf gives orders to Speer, but Albert drags his feet in carrying them out. Some of the other ministers and generals are close to panic."

"You must do something, Joseph. Adolf is our friend." She put her hand on mine as if to urge me to action.

"What can I do, Magda? His last order to me was to gather a citizen's army to defend Berlin. I did so, cajoling and threatening until I managed barely two-thirds of a regiment, but don't look too closely: they are old men and young boys, for that is all I could muster from what is left of the male Berliners."

"You are sending them to their deaths!"

"No, no. I housed them in a warehouse at the southern outskirts, told them to wait for orders. My hope is that the British reach them first and take them prisoner. I wanted to keep them away from the Soviet murderers."

"So, there is no hope?" Magda asked. Her voice was cool and even.

"For Adolf? He wants none. He will not attempt escape. He will not fight for fear of being captured and disgraced. He has accepted defeat and intends only to die. But what of us, Magda?" I gripped her hand. "What do we decide?"

For a moment, Magda seemed to be in a daydream. She blinked her eyes. "Let us first get the children to the safety of the bunker and then decide there what we will do."

We slept in the children's rooms that night, I with the three oldest and Magda with the three youngest. We helped each other to lay bedding on the floor, then hugged and bid each other a good night's sleep. Every time I drifted off, my night terrors began to take shape like fade-in scenes from a dark movie. I would jerk awake, rub my eyes, and stare at the blank ceiling until I began to fall asleep again.

The nannies roused us at seven, and the servants indicated that they had packed our clothes and personal things for the move to the bunker. We were given a hamper of fresh food, and the children were allowed two personal items apiece. All the girls chose favorite toys or dolls. Helmut, all of nine years old, solemnly chose a set of crayons and his favorite book, *Der Strewwelpeter* by Heinrich Hoffman.

"Helmut, no!" Magda complained. She thought the Hoffman book, a collection of cautionary tales about what happens to naughty children, morbid.

Helmut clutched the slim book to his chest. "Was a present to me," he insisted. In fact, I had read it as a child myself and then read it to my son when he was just four. He enjoyed, as much as I did, the stories of children whose bad behavior was dealt with radically, such as Konrad, whose thumb-sucking is curtailed by a wandering tailor who cuts off the boy's thumbs.

"Let it go, Magda," I said quietly. I patted Helmut's head. "It's fine, my son."

By eight, we were bundled into two cars and speeding through Berlin to the bunker under the Chancellery. We arrived without incident, although the children, unused to the sound of artillery fire, hugged each other and held hands. Once inside, however, they were more interested in exploring the vast warren of rooms of the upper bunker. "There's more to explore," I teased. "Tomorrow, perhaps, you will see the lower floor and the garden."

Karl Gebhardt, the head of the German Red Cross, pulled me aside. "I can take the children out of the city under the auspices of my office."

I shook my head. "Magda and I have already decided that the children will stay with us."

"Then, let me take you and Mrs. Goebbels as well. I will have fake identities made for you."

"You are suggesting that I commit treason, Karl, running from the Führer when he most needs me." I turned to walk away. I did not trust Gebhardt despite his reputation as a gifted doctor; there were stories about horrific experiments he carried out on prisoners at Ravensbrück concentration camp.

"Your children," was all he said.

After lunch, Magda and I agreed that we should see Adolf. Our cook, Lottie, had packed some eclairs for him, one of his favorite desserts, and it was our perfect excuse to see how he was doing. Our eldest, Helga, insisted on coming along because she knew that Adolf always allowed her to sit in his lap, but when we reached the dark staircase that descended to the lower bunker, she refused to go farther, so we sent her back to our rooms.

"Ah, Magda and Joseph! I am so glad to see you," Adolf said, rising from his desk. We had reached his office, which was crowded with a desk, three office chairs, and a phone. Next door was the radio room where messages could be sent and received, as well as a bulky transmission machine for broadcasting to the public.

Magda allowed Adolf to hug her while I clapped him on his arm amiably. "We wanted to let you know we are here with the children and will stay as long as necessary," Magda said. "Here," she added, handing him the plate of three eclairs. "You should refrigerate these."

"Who's to say I won't eat them immediately," Adolf answered, placing the plate on his desk. But when he sat down, his smile and genial manner seemed to disappear.

"Forgive me, but you look tired, Adolf," Magda said and reached for his hand.

Adolf, however, quickly put his hand in his jacket pocket. "I have not been sleeping well with all the noise outside."

I looked at Magda, my eyes indicating that I had noticed how he'd hidden his trembling hand. "Please have your doctor give you a light sleeping potion," I suggested.

Adolf nodded. "Joseph, I am not going out any longer. The army betrays me by not repulsing the advancing Soviets. I cannot be captured and mocked." He bit his upper lip. "Also, my throat is so dry in this bunker. Will you take over the daily radio broadcasts?"

He was referring to the half-hour or so that he spoke on the radio to all of the Germans who still had access to our broadcasting. His last message was the day before his birthday. "Of course, my Führer," I replied. "It would be my honor."

He pointed to a framed oil portrait above his desk. "Do you know who this is?"

"A great ruler," I answered. "Frederick the Great. Barbarossa."

Adolf winced at the word *barbarossa*, perhaps a painful reminder of Germany's failure to conquer Russia. "Yes. Did you know that he, too, was defeated by an army of Russians?" He shook his head sadly.

I said nothing. Magda turned away, unwilling to see the regret in Adolf's eyes.

"I thought I could learn from his mistakes. I wonder if his lieutenants were faithful." He took a breath. "Bormann is always running off to do something or other, Speer comes and goes at will, and both Göring and Hesse have left to attend to their duties. I rely on you."

I suspected that both Bormann and Speer were arranging for their own departures from the bunker, and even without concrete evidence, I sensed that Göring and Hesse had already deserted us. "I will prepare something and get your approval before each broadcast."

"No need for approvals anymore. I am busy preparing my papers for posterity." He cleared his throat. "Now," he smiled weakly, "I'm afraid I will ask your leave for me to rest a bit. I'll just take these sweets to Eva. They will be our dessert tonight."

Magda and I left, smiling and trying to sound cheerful. When we reached the top of the stairs, I said quietly, "It is worse than I imagined."

We had been in the bunker for a little over a week. The novelty of the place lasted only a few days for the children, but once they were allowed time aboveground in the bunker garden, they adapted to the new routine. Their favorite activity was playing with Adolf's dog, Blondi.

Magda busied herself by overseeing the considerable number of staff in the bunker, a task that Eva was unwilling to assume; she preferred to remain in her room listening to records. I noted that of all of Adolf's high-ranking officials, only Martin Bormann and I remained. Others had either never appeared or had left soon after the Führer's birthday. Those who quietly slipped away before the end of April included Albert Bormann (Martin's younger brother), von Ribbentrop (who escaped to Munich), Theodor Morell (Adolf's physician), and Albert Speer, who had previously, Magda said, begged her several times to allow him to take our children somewhere "to safety."

Still, on April 28th, there were more than two dozen staff crowded into the upper and lower bunkers, mostly medical and administrative. The atmosphere sometimes became oppressive especially because there were daily air raids. Nevertheless, we all tried to remain civil and upbeat.

In the late afternoon, I was editing my ten-minute broadcast for that evening when one of the adjutants told me that Hitler required my presence. He had kept to his private rooms for the past few days, and it was only through Bormann did we know that he was all right. I hurried to his office but was directed instead to his sitting room.

"Are you all right?" I asked.

"Yes, Joseph. I am fine. But I want your help with this matter." He waved to the others in the room – Bormann, Eva, two nurses, and Gerda Christian (one of his secretaries) – to leave while ordering Traudl Junge, his chief secretary, to remain. "I am composing my will. It will be in two parts: a political and a personal testament. I want you to be the editor, please." He motioned me to sit next to him.

For the next few hours, we sat together and went over his notes. I offered a few corrections, mostly suggesting additional comments to clarify some items. When we were done, around nine p.m., Adolf said he would dictate the formal document to Frau Junge while I was to gather my wife, Bormann, and some others to meet him after midnight in his private quarters.

"Why are we to see him after midnight?" Magda asked me. "Did he tell you?"

"I spent the last few hours helping him complete his last will and testament, Magda. Traudl is probably typing it up now. I presume he just wants us to witness the document."

"So he expects to die," she said quietly.

"You need to know this, Magda. He has detailed in the document his plans for the government upon his death as well as who is to succeed him."

She did not speak, but I saw her teeth clench.

"Karl Dönitz is to be president, Bormann party minister, and I, Chancellor." I bowed my head.

"What you dreamed of, Joseph, chancellor."

"Once, yes."

"And now?"

"These are his orders, Magda. Dare I refuse?" Becoming chancellor on Adolf's death seemed wrong to me somehow. "We will talk after our meeting with him."

We were surprised when we were led into the map room and saw Adolf with Eva beside him. She was holding a small spray of flowers from the garden. "You are my witnesses," Adolf said with a grim smile. "I finally succumb!" he added jovially and turned to the lawyer who had been hurriedly found to officiate. "Let's go."

When we emerged from the room, Eva held out her hand to show her wedding ring to the two secretaries standing there. They immediately hugged her and congratulated her. Adolf said, "Magda, please excuse us now. We men have important business that cannot wait." He ushered us back into the map room, kissing Eva briefly on the cheek.

"Martin," Adolf said, "you and Joseph will witness this document as my true and final will and testament." He handed a fountain pen to Martin who uncapped the pen and leaned over the desk. "You may look it over, but Joseph and I have already completed it. There will be no changes."

"You may think of something tomorrow or in a few weeks," Martin said.

"I intend to die tonight. I refuse to surrender or be taken alive. I do this for Germany."

Martin looked at me. I nodded and said, "Please witness this document, Martin. Our Führer insists."

When we completed the signing and left the map room, Adolf joined Eva, and they retired to his sitting room, first saying goodbye to those gathered in the lower bunker. Eva gave her fur coat to one of the secretaries. Adolf shook hands with everyone, making sure to say something personal to each person. Then, they disappeared into his quarters.

When they were gone, Martin turned to me. "I ask only once more. Shall I take your children to safety? Will you and Magda come with me?"

I shook my head.

"I do not think we will meet again. Goodbye, Joseph." He didn't shake my hand or give me a brotherly hug. He simply turned on his heel and headed for the staircase.

"Go to the children. I'll be along momentarily," I said to Magda, who immediately obeyed me. "You are all released from your duties," I said to the remaining crowd. Most left, many of the women weeping quietly.

My personal guards remained with me. We heard a muffled shot and looked at one another. "Look inside and report to me." I looked at my watch to note the time: 2 a.m., April 30.

One of the guards returned and said, "He has shot himself to the right temple. Frau Eva is also dead. Cyanide, I think, because there is a smell of almonds."

"Take the bodies to the garden. Be respectful of our leader. Bring enough petrol to burn them as the Führer commanded, then meet me in my quarters." I went upstairs.

"Magda, do you wish to go back home?"

She sat at a small table, looking at her hands. "I should have gotten a manicure," she said absently. Then, "No, Joseph. What world will it be without Adolf?"

"How shall we handle the children?"

"I've thought much about this. You told me how you are reborn from earlier lives. Perhaps the children can be reborn into a world where someone like Hitler governs once again, and their future will be bright. Perhaps I, too, can be reborn."

"If only we could know," I said. "My knowledge was, for so long, a terrible burden. Now, it is my cause for hope. I have been fortunate to know my past, but I know nothing of the future. I still have much to do, I think."

Magda opened her hands and showed me six cyanide tablets. "The dentist, Helmut Kunz, gave these to me."

"For the children," I said. "Have Kunz give them morphine first, enough to make them cooperative."

"He's waiting in his rooms. I'll fetch him. What of Göring and Himmler? Have they returned?"

"Cowards," I muttered. "Adolf has disowned them in his testament, stripped them of all ranks and awards. Denounced them as traitors to the Reich." I shrugged. "Let's get the children."

It was 4 a.m., and the children were cranky because we'd awakened them. After Kunz injected each with a small dose of morphine ("It's your energy shot," he told them jovially), we gave each a cyanide tablet. "Your vitamin," Magda said with a smile.

"Who can chew it the fastest?" I asked.

My dear son, Helmut, was the first to shout, "Me!" and the girls raised their hands enthusiastically. Except Helga, the oldest. As the rest chewed, they slumped back down onto their beds; their eyes fluttered closed, and they were still.

Helga began to cough and choke. "I don't like this," she said, putting her finger in her mouth to retrieve the tablet fragments.

"No, Helga, you must swallow it," Magda said, grabbing her daughter's hands.

"I don't want it!" Helga protested, trying to get out of bed.

I leaned on her, pinning her shoulders. "Swallow it, my dear, please."

"No!" She struggled against me and started to spit.

I clamped her jaw shut with my hand and pressed hard. "Swallow it!" I heard a soft crack; I had dislocated her jaw, and she started to dribble. "Close your eyes, Helga. Relax. Swallow." Dribble started to run from the corner of her mouth. Tears sprang up in her eyes as she gasped for air. "My darling daughter," I said, still gripping her jaw.

A few moments later, Magda touched my hand. "She's gone," she said. "Let's tuck her in with the rest."

"The sun will be up soon. Why don't we go to the garden?" I suggested. Before we left our rooms, I said to my adjutant, "Wait ten minutes, then bring petrol to the garden. Make sure that my wife and I leave nothing but ashes for the communists to find."

Magda put on her wool coat against the morning chill, and I straightened my tie and jacket. "Our last stroll together, Magda!" I said brightly as we headed outside. "You must go first so I can be sure that you are safely gone, dearest. Don't wait for me."

"I don't want it to hurt," she said, trembling.

I grinned. "You must allow me a literary allusion, my dear: 'The stroke of death is as a lover's pinch, which hurts and is desired,' said Shakespeare's Cleopatra." I pinched her arm.

We found a bench, and I gave Magda the cyanide tablet. "You will smell like my favorite marzipan candy, my darling. Look up at the sky and the rising sun." When Magda gently leaned against me, lifeless, the scent of almonds heavy on her, I took the Dionysus coin from my pocket and held it up to the sun, its irregular disc like a golden eclipse. "Devotion has been my excess," I whispered into Magda's hair, hoping that the spirit within me would escape before the guards came with the petrol. I thought I could taste my mother's *bienenstich kuchen* – bee sting cake with its crunchy honey-almond topping – as I bit down on the tablet in my mouth.

www.ingramcontent.com/pod-product-compliance
Lightning Source LLC
Chambersburg PA
CBHW031456160726
47994CB00005B/2064